BUSINESS WARRIOR

How to use the SWIPPE™ method to survive, prosper and dominate in business.

RECESSION & RECOVERY EDITION

By

Adrian Gluck, PhD

Visit www.businesswarriorinstitute.com to order additional copies and for information on the Business Warrior Institute.

ABOUT THE AUTHOR

Adrian Gluck began his career with Exxon Corporation. He then became chief information officer for a large insurance company, after which he launched a computer software company that became the leading provider of auto fleet leasing systems with worldwide clients including Avis and Hertz. Subsequently, Gluck was founder, director, and advisor to several companies. Many of these companies now have market values in excess of $100 million. Most of them dominate their markets, and all have benefitted from Gluck's proprietary SWIPPE™ system. Gluck holds patents and patents pending for several technologies including trading cards, memorabilia, fan photography, digital imaging, mapping systems, Web indexing, and e-commerce systems. His technologies have helped generate sales of over $3 billion to date. Gluck is president of Media Technologies Licensing LLC, a patent licensing company; managing partner at Moriah Partners, a private equity investment firm; president of Kinter Management Inc., a management consulting company; and a senior advisor to Business Warrior Institute LLC, an advanced strategic training institute. Gluck holds industrial engineering, MBA and PhD degrees, and he is a registered professional engineer.

✳ ✳ ✳

DEDICATIONS

To the memory of my mother and my father who survived the
Holocaust and Communist Romania and inspired me to go to
America, get an education, work hard, and make a difference

✼ ✼ ✼

To my amazing wife, Susan, who has always believed in me,
no matter how crazy the ideas, how lofty the dreams and
how big the sacrifices

✼ ✼ ✼

To my wonderful children and biggest fans – Leslie, Stacey,
Carla, Jonathan, and Michael, and my granddaughter Hannah,
for making it all worthwhile

✼ ✼ ✼

To the United States of America, the promised land in my
childhood dreams, that made those dreams come true and gave
me more than I could ever repay

✼ ✼ ✼

CONTENTS

✧ ✧ ✧

WARNINGS

The tactics presented in this book were developed to be used ethically. Power nailers can shoot hundreds of nails per minute to build great buildings but may be misused to shoot someone in the head instead. So too the tactics in this book can enable you to do great good faster and better for your business, but could be unethical when used for evil purposes.

☆ ☆ ☆

The information, ideas, and suggestions in this book are not intended to render professional advice. Before using any of the information, ideas, and suggestions contained in this book, you should consult your personal advisors. Neither the author nor the publisher shall be liable for any loss or damage allegedly arising as a consequence of your use of any information, ideas, and suggestions in this book.

☆ ☆ ☆

☆ ☆ ☆

ACKNOWLEDGMENTS

As has been said, we're all dwarfs standing on the shoulders of giants. I am deeply indebted to a great number of people who let me stand on their shoulders and taught me much of what I know by challenging, inspiring, and trusting me. The list must start with my wife, Susan, our family's "sergeant major," without whom my life would have fallen into anarchy a long time ago. I must also thank my brother Gilbert, whose love of books and incessant quest for knowledge have taught me from an early age that books are to be cherished and learning is a lifelong pursuit. Many thanks to my son Jonathan, a successful entrepreneur in his own right and a trusted advisor, who has helped make this book relevant to the twenty- and thirty-somethings generation. Many thanks are deserved by Evan Pinchuk, my wonderful son-in-law and the president of Business Warrior Institute LLC, who is always ready to do whatever needs to be done and finds solutions to problems no matter how thorny they may be. He has shed important insights that have vastly improved this book. Last but not least, I must thank Joseph Konowiecki, successful attorney, business executive, entrepreneur, and my co-managing partner at Moriah Partners LLC. For the past twenty years, he has been a great friend, advisor, and wonderful partner in many worthwhile business and community projects.

✵ ✵ ✵

INTRODUCTION

A good introduction is like a good honeymoon – you never want it to end.
– Anonymous

Why I Wrote This Book

During the many years I have travelled through the wonderful world called business, I experienced many spectacular successes and some not-so-spectacular failures. For a while now, I felt the time has come to share my experiences with others by writing a book. As the world of business is much too vast and complex to cover in a single book, I had to select one business "land" that could be of most interest to the largest number of readers. I believe I found such a land: the mysterious land of *recessions*.

Why I Chose Recessions as the Topic

One reason I wrote this book is that at this time (2009), we are mired in the deepest recession since the Great Depression of 1929–1939. Another is that while the topics of what recessions are and how governments can help us get out of them have been well covered in literature, the topic of *how businesses should deal with recessions* has been largely unexplored. Finally, over the years, I have developed SWIPPE™, a recession-battling system that has been so wildly successful that I now feel confident it can be widely used in most business settings.

Businesses spend one-quarter of their lives in recession and another quarter of their lives before and after recessions worrying about recessions, preparing for recessions, and recovering from recessions. As a result, *businesses are mired in a recessionary mind-set about half of their lives.* In other words:

Businesses spend about half their lives in recessionary times.

So what, you may ask? Well, the problem with this picture is that recessionary mind-sets are very bad for a business's health. Their ugly sidekicks are *defeatism, scapegoating, criticism, cynicism,* and, worst of all, *fear.* Their sad results are *loss of customers, loss of jobs,* and even *bankruptcy.*

What This Book Covers

The book introduces SWIPPE™, a highly successful recession-fighting system developed and battle-tested on tens of businesses over the past several years. SWIPPE™ enables businesses to survive, prosper, and beat recessions before recessions beat *them.* SWIPPE™ empowers businesses to take advantage of recessions and beat their competition to gain market share. The most visible impact of SWIPPE™ is the rapid change of a business's mind-set from *self-defeating negativity* to *empowerment.*

What This Book Does Not Cover

This book is *not* about learning how recessions get started or how to prevent them. These topics have been covered by hundreds and hundreds of books, studies, and articles taking every imaginable point of view. Most of these agree that there is not much an individual business can do to either prevent or stop recessions. Our top economists, the Congress and our presidents have never been able to stop recessions from happening. For the foreseeable future, recessions will be a fact of life. They are here to stay, and businesses better learn how to deal with them, else they too may become recession roadkill during this recession or the next one, just like hundreds of thousands of businesses before them.

There are hundreds and hundreds of business theories, strategies, and tactics explained and dissected in thousands upon thousands of business books. While many are worthwhile, most have no empirical basis; they are based merely on opinions, hearsay, and conjecture. Unlike those books, unless I have personally developed, applied, or experienced a tactic firsthand, I did not include it in the SWIPPE™ system; and therefore, it is not included in this book.

I tried to make this book a quick and easy read. Each of the six missions of SWIPPE™ is described in detail, and lots of examples are given in order to make these missions' tactics easy to understand. If after reading the book you would like to learn more, please go to www.businesswarriorinstitute.com for additional information.

Recessions have a habit of fully entering our consciousness rather suddenly, relentlessly, and with a vengeance. One day our customers are happy, our business is going well, and our employees are positive; the next, we start hearing a recession may be coming, sales start going down, and our employees are in the doldrums. By the time we take appropriate measures – if we even know for sure what they should be – it may be too late. Thus, no moment should be spared from reading this book, then jumping into the fray and beating the recessions down, down, down!

I hope you will have as much fun reading this book as I had writing it.

Adrian Gluck, BASc, PE, MBA, PhD

Beverly Hills, California
April 2009

BACKGROUND

CHAPTER 1
Introduction to the SWIPPE™ System

The expert in battle seeks his victory from strategic advantage and does not demand it from his men.

– Sun Tzu (722–221 BC), Chinese general
and author of the book The Art of War

Introduction

This chapter introduces the basics of the SWIPPE™ recession-battling system, its six key combatants and its six battle missions.

✩ ✩ ✩

The Killer Product

The SWIPPE™ system helps business entrepreneurs, owners, and managers *survive and prosper during recessions.* If properly used, the system enables them to "swippe" significant market share from key competitors. SWIPPE™ opens them up to *unique opportunities for growth not available during nonrecessionary times.* At its best, SWIPPE™ can make business entrepreneurs, owners, and managers *the dominant players in their marketplace.*

To parallel what the quote from Sun Tzu above says, businesses cannot expect to win competitive battles mainly on the shoulders of their employees. Unfortunately, that is what most business leaders do; they demand ever-increasing commitments and sacrifices from their employees while ignoring a much, much more important element of winning: having *a unique strategic advantage created by a killer product.* Contrary to popular belief in business circles, while having good employees is indeed an important part of winning, it is *not the most important part.*

The single most important thing I have personally learned over the thirty or so years I have been practicing *strategic positioning* – the science that answers the question "what business should we be in?" – is this:

Succeeding during recessions has less to do with having the capital, equipment, facilities, and good people, and more to do with having a

killer product.

While obtaining enough capital, buying the latest equipment, relocating to better facilities, and hiring great people would be very helpful, Business Warriors cannot normally fully accomplish these objectives during the short eighteen months or so the typical recession lasts. They must *choose the most important objective and make absolutely sure it is accomplished*. During recessions, the principal objective they must choose is *creating and successfully deploying a killer product*. This book shows how to use the SWIPPE™ system to consistently create such killer products and how to deploy them successfully to fairly and squarely "kill" the key competitors' product sales. Most importantly, the SWIPPE™ system enables entrepreneurs and established businesses alike to Win With Honor™ over their key competitors.

The Six Missions of SWIPPE™

SWIPPE™ is an acronym made up of the key words describing the six "missions" making up the SWIPPE™ system: *strengths, weaknesses, ideal mission, product, protection, and execution*. The six missions that make up the SWIPPE™ system are the following:

- **Mission 1**: Determine the *Strengths* of Business Warrior's current product.

- **Mission 2**: Find the *Weaknesses* of the key competing product.

- **Mission 3**: Develop the *Ideal Objective* to be accomplished.

- **Mission 4**: Create a new *Product* that embodies the *Ideal Objective*.

- **Mission 5**: *Protect* the new *Product* against the competition.

- **Mission 6**: *Execute* the battle plan and accomplish the *Ideal Objective*.

The following diagram shows the SWIPPE™ system's six missions in the order in which they must be carried out:

The Six Missions of the SWIPPE™ System

© 2009 Business Warrior Institute LLC

The Six Key Combatants

As with all other human activities, when it comes to business competition battles, it is of vital importance to understand the wants, needs, and behaviors of the various participants. Several chapters in this book are dedicated to doing just that. The diagram below shows who the key participants in the SWIPPE™ system are and the relationships between them. In order to bring home the point that *the SWIPPE™ system is all about waging war on the Business Warrior's key competitors,* we refer to its participants as combatants. To better understand the role played by each key combatant, it is useful to see what their military equivalents are; hence, they are in **bold** for emphasis:

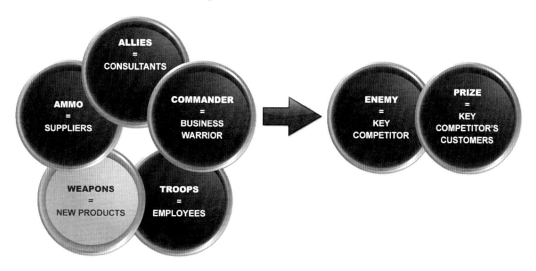

The SWIPPE™ System's Six Key Combatants

© 2009 Business Warrior Institute LLC

We will also learn the key tactics to:

A. enhance the effectiveness of the combatants fighting on the side of the Business Warriors while

B. diminishing the effectiveness of Business Warriors' key competitors.

Many other books, articles, seminars, and experts suggest that during recessions, it is best to pull in your horns, lay low, and not make waves. If you want to take this passive- defensive approach, stop reading this book right now, and good luck; the SWIPPE™ system is *not* for you. If, on the other hand, you don't want to be a victim but a victor and you don't want to be a follower but want to be a leader, then SWIPPE™ is your answer.

The SWIPPE™ system is not for the timid and the indecisive. To implement it successfully requires acceptance of the following stark reality: *during recessions, the normal rules of business must be thrown out the door, and new ones must be adopted.* To accomplish this, you must start by learning what those new rules are. This is what the SWIPPE™ system delivers, and this book will show you how to do it.

✵ ✵ ✵

CHAPTER 2
About Recessions

Recession is when your neighbor loses his job.
Depression is when you lose yours.

– Ronald Reagan (1911–2004), fortieth president of the
United States and thirty-third governor of California

Introduction

In this chapter, we will learn about recessions: what they are, how they get started, how often they occur, and how long they last. Recessions are unfortunate times when most of us feel overwhelmed by economic losses. As consumers, we lose our power to buy all the things we were planning to buy; as employees, we lose our ability to ask for that overdue raise, and maybe even worse, our jobs; and as businesspeople, we lose sales, profits, market share, and sometimes even our companies. The emotional impact is made worse by the fact that *many of us were never even in the "fight" that led to the recession.* We lost a fight we never even fought. Most of us didn't increase prices exorbitantly, didn't trade in futures, and didn't short-sell stocks. Most of us didn't export jobs overseas, and we certainly didn't package mortgages into exotic security instruments that during the recession started in 2008 became "toxic."

FACT 1 Businesses don't have a clue what to do during recessions.

Most businesspeople don't *exactly* know *what steps to take during a recession, when to take them, and how to take them* with a minimum of disruption. "Should we lower our prices?" "Should we reduce our staff?" "Should we increase advertising?" "Should we decrease advertising?" And so on. As a result, most end up acting on instincts, gut feelings, and hunches. Or they just do what their competitors are doing. What they *don't* do is follow a system. Businesses have detailed business plans for the "good times," but rarely for recessions.

This lack of recession planning is due to most businesspeople's lack of understanding of recessions' dynamics. It is like throwing a birthday party versus planning a funeral. We are all pretty good at throwing parties, but when it comes to funerals, we don't have a clue what to do. That's why there are so many well-established funeral operators while party planning is mostly a cottage industry.

This lack of recession know-how is not totally our fault. Standard business education does not prepare us for recessions. Virtually everything we learn in undergraduate and graduate-level business courses is based on the assumption that business companies operate in a healthy economy, as if bad times never happened. We are taught how to build, operate, account, and market during the good times *in between recessions*. Unfortunately, we are not taught how to make decisions during the "bad times," the times *during the recessions*. There is so little thought given to recessions that *there are no specific courses on recession offered by any of our leading business schools*.

To make matters worse, business media does not inform us about the details of recessions beyond the usual macroeconomic rantings and ravings that seem to endlessly captivate viewers, listeners, and readers. Recessions are not fun to write about, and few of us like reading, listening to, or watching negative economic news.

How about finding recession courses using the Web? Amazingly, if you google the terms "courses on recession," "course on recession," "recession courses," or "business courses on recession," you get zero results! By way of contrast, "economics courses" returns 138,000 results, "statistics courses" returns 104,000, "finance courses" returns 109,000, and "marketing courses" returns 259,000 results.

It is important to understand something about the workings of recessions, and the following is a short introduction to the subject.

FACT 2 Recessions are significant *declines in economic activity.*

The National Bureau of Economic Research defines a recession as "a significant decline in economic activity spread across the economy, lasting more than a few months, normally visible in real Gross Domestic Product, real income, employment, industrial production and wholesale-retail sales." A popular rule of thumb is that a recession takes place if the gross domestic product (GDP) growth is negative for two or more consecutive quarters – that is, six or more months.

Recessions are national economic phenomena – that is, they happen across most of the economy at the same time. However, due to the natural cyclicality of business, slowdowns and downturns take place fairly regularly within most industries, separate and apart from the rest of the economy. In fact, nearly *20% of all U.S. industries battle downturns in any given year.* When that happens, most of us don't hear about it. It only affects those involved in those industries: its employees, customers, suppliers, and investors. For example, when oil prices go through the roof, the auto and airline industries typically go through industry recessions. When copper prices soar, the electrical wiring industry has a recession, and so on. Because these industry recessions are of no broad interest to the public, the mainstream media doesn't report them ad nauseam the way they do when national recessions occur. Yet for the business managers, employees, and investors in the affected industries, these are real recessions presenting them with serious live-or-die situations. For these reasons, this book's learnings are applicable not only to national recessions but also to industry-specific recessions.

FACT 3 Recessions have *winners and losers.*

Like most struggles in life, recessions have winners and losers. If you read this book in 2008/2009, you are in the middle of a recession of historic proportions. Tens of thousands of jobs are being lost, and businesses across the country are headed for extinction. But like so many recessions before it, most companies will survive this recession unscathed, thousands of employees and managers will get promotions, and millions of consumers will profit from lower prices, better services, and wider merchandise choices.

Winners and losers emerge from every contest and economic change. There are losers when times get tough, but there are also winners. There are many opportunities during recessions that are not available to the average business during nonrecessionary times. *Someone is going to seize those opportunities, gather up the customers others aren't taking care of, and invent new ways to corner new markets and profit from them. That someone might as well be you.*

EXAMPLE A Star Is Born

I first experienced the phenomenon of an industry doing better during a recession than before it during the 1975–1977 recession. The United States was saddled with double-digit inflation and soaring gas prices due to an oil embargo caused by another Middle East crisis. I had recently left my position of chief information officer at a large insurance company and launched my own software company. Due to the recession, companies large and small needed to conserve capital and reduce their monthly costs. In order to accomplish this, companies were increasingly outsourcing their software development, which created opportunities for software companies like mine. In addition, in order to conserve precious capital, more and more companies started leasing their auto fleets instead of buying them. As a result, during the recession of 1975–1977, the auto leasing industry grew to unprecedented levels.

I took advantage of both of these trends and launched my own company that eventually dominated the market for computerized auto leasing systems with worldwide clients including both Avis and Hertz.

FACT 4 Downturns, crashes, depressions, and panics are *recessions*.

There is some confusion about the terminology used when referring to economic downturns. Many economic downturns have been called recessions, some recessions have been called depressions, and a few depressions have been categorized as panics. Why so many different names? Primarily because recessions don't start suddenly; they develop gradually over periods of months, and even years. At their inception, they are downturns, and at their troughs, depending on their severity, they are referred to as recessions if they are the garden-variety type – a couple of percentage points contraction in the gross national product (GNP) – or crashes, depressions, and panics if the economic contraction is more severe. To make it easier, *in this book, we will refer to all business down cycles – be they downturns, recessions, crashes, depressions, or panics – simply as recessions.* Keep in mind that there are also recessions that affect only certain industries, independent of the economy at large. The learnings of this book are applicable to such industry recessions as well.

FACT 5 The American economy is in nonrecessionary times *only about one-half of the time.*

Here are some important statistics about recessions:

- Since World War II (1939–1945), the average recession has lasted about eighteen months.

- The average time between recessions has been fifty-seven months.

- The American economy is in recession about one-fourth of the time and in recessionary times pre- and post-recessions another one-fourth of the time.

- The American economy is in nonrecessionary times only about one-half of the time.

- The average company profits drop by 30% during recessions.

- Only about 15% of the one thousand U.S. industries are recession-proof. (For a list of industries most likely to be recession-proof, see appendix 2).

From these statistics, it should be clear that recessions are *very* important business phenomena. This is especially so because, unless tended to, almost everything of importance to a business changes during recessions: demand for its products, the prices customers are willing to pay for its products, its cost of capital, the aging of its account receivables, its cost of materials, and more.

EXAMPLE A Highly Recommended Restaurant

Say you wanted to eat at a restaurant that is highly rated by a respected food critic, but found out that on average, one-quarter of the people eating at that restaurant get food poisoning. Would you still eat there? Would you ever trust that critic again? Most likely not. How about finding out that the car you have wanted for so long, which is highly recommended by *Consumer Reports*, in actuality breaks down a quarter of the time. Would you take a 1-in-4 chance that every time you drove it you would get stuck, possibly on a busy freeway on the way to work? Would you still buy it? Would you still trust *Consumer Reports*? Unlikely. Yet this is the reality facing you when it comes to recessions: chances are, you will be spending a *quarter of your business life battling recessions*. Yet you have not been trained for recessions. There are virtually no expert recession advisers that can help you, and you cannot rely on your normal business information sources.

FACT 6 There *are* recession-proof industries.

Only about 15% of the one thousand industries tracked by economists are recession-proof or somewhat recession-proof. Goods and services produced by recession-proof industries have a low income elasticity of demand, and thus business involving these goods remains relatively stable despite the fall in discretionary income that occurs during an economic recession. Most recession-proof industries produce soft goods, which are necessities that buyers need regardless of the economic conditions prevailing in the marketplace. Even during a recession, people need to wear clothes, have shelter, feed themselves, and take care of their safety and health. These are everyday necessities that never go away. These industries are in contrast to those that produce high-priced durable goods and luxury goods such as automobiles and jewelry.

As further proof that not all industries suffer during recessions, here is a list of major companies hiring in 2009 despite the recession, according to CareerBuilder.com:

- 7-Eleven

- Banfield

- Farmers Insurance

- Gentiva Health Services

- HealthMarkets

- ITT

- M.A.R.S. International

- PricewaterhouseCoopers

- ServiceMaster

- State Farm Insurance

- Sutter Health

- The Scotts Miracle-Gro Company

- URS Corporation

FACT 7 Recessions happen with *great regularity*.

I will be referring throughout the book to the most recent recessions, those of 1975–1977, 1980–1982, 1990–1992, 2000–2002, and the current one that started in 2008. It would probably be instructive to take a look at a summary description of these recessions and the troughs of all the American recessions, both listed in appendix 3. As you will see, there were numerous recessions, and they have been happening with regularity. Even though many pundits and wishful thinkers at the end of some of the recessions pronounced that there will never be another recession, they have been proven wrong over and over. It appears certain that despite recession-abatement measures introduced by the United States Congress and the federal government, the economic swings will continue for the foreseeable future. The overwhelming likelihood is that there will be many more recessions in the future.

CHAPTER 3
Great Opportunities

The pessimist sees difficulty in every opportunity.
The optimist sees the opportunity in every difficulty.

– Sir Winston Churchill (1874–1965), prime minister of United Kingdom,
military officer, historian, Nobel Prize–winning writer and artist

Introduction

In this chapter, we are introducing a startling finding: recessions *can be very good for business!* We will look back in history and see how great fortunes were made by businesses that took advantage of the opportunities that opened up due to the economic turmoil surrounding wars. We will then analyze a number of opportunities created by recessions.

✵ ✵ ✵

FACT 1 Recessions *intensify* the raging business wars that are always going on.

Recessions are times of strife and stress. Nothing seems to remain the same as most people and businesses are affected in one way or another. Commerce slows down. The cost of certain goods goes through the roof, while the cost of others deflates to levels not normally seen. Most of us tighten our belt and conserve our cash. Luxuries go out the door. Lenders rein in their lending. The government intervenes to protect the population from the economic ravages of the recession and undertakes extraordinary actions, including taking control of entire swaths of the economy.

This is not unlike what happens to an economy during wartime. As you will see in later chapters, business marketing is often likened to and modeled after war strategies and tactics. Since the military has had many more centuries to hone their skills in crisis management than civilian institutions, let's see how we may benefit from drawing parallels between wars and recessions.

EXAMPLE World War I Riches

The title of a *New York Times* article appearing on October 1, 1915, shortly after the start of World War I (1914–1918) read,

> SUDDEN FORTUNES MADE IN WALL ST.; Speculators in War Stocks Gain Rapid Wealth as Prices Go Soaring. $500,000 ON $650 START Investor Who Put $18,000 Into Bethlehem for His Baby Has $364,000 for Youngster.

In the seminal book *War is a Racket,* written by the two-time Congressional Medal of Honor recipient Marine Corp major general Smedley D. Butler, the author counts that at least twenty-one thousand new millionaires were made in the United States during World War I. He enumerates the wealth created by that war among leading American companies of the time:

- *DuPont Corporation* average earnings for the period 1910 to 1914 were $6 million a year. Their average yearly profit during the war years, 1914 to 1918, was $58 million, an increase in profits of more than 950%.

- *Bethlehem Steel* promptly turned to munitions making during World War I. Prior to that, their yearly earnings averaged $6 million. Their 1914–1918 average was $49 million a year.

- *United States Steel*'s normal earnings during the five-year period prior to World War I were $105 million a year. Then along came the war, and up went the profits. The average yearly profit for the period 1914–1918 was $240 million.

- *Anaconda*'s average yearly earnings during the prewar years, 1910–1914, were $10 million. During the war years, 1914–1918, profits leaped to $34 million a year.

- *Utah Copper*'s average of $5 million profit per year during the 1910–1914 period jumped to an average of $21 million in yearly profits for the 1914–1918 World War I time span.

- *International Nickel Company* showed an increase in profits from a mere average of $4 million a year to $73 million yearly.

- *American Sugar Refining Company* averaged $2 million a year for the three years before the war. In 1916, a profit of $6 million was recorded.

EXAMPLE Iraqi War Riches

- Kellogg Brown & Root, a subsidiary of Halliburton, was awarded a contract to provide all the logistical and maintenance needs of U.S. forces in Iraq. This contract is expandable up to $7 billion.

- Bechtel is the number one construction contractor in the U.S. It collected over $680 million from the U.S. Agency for International Development (USAID) for eighteen months of infrastructure construction in Iraq.

FACT 2 Recessions present *unique business opportunities.*

Just as during wartime, recessions present rare and unique business opportunities. During the good times, in between recessions, as during times of peace, money flows freely and fuels the launch of new products and new companies. During recessions, the money flow slows down to a trickle. Cash and credit are tight. Weak companies go out of business, and large, established companies freeze expenditures on new products and new features for existing products.

Yet despite these dire conditions, my own experiences and those of many others show that *recessions can be very good for businesses.* First and foremost, they provide businesses a unique opportunity to improve their position vis-à-vis that of their competitors. While their competitors are paralyzed in fear, forward-thinking businesses and entrepreneurs seek opportunities. While competitors cut back on product development, staff, and facilities, these mavericks launch new products, increase their staff, and add new facilities.

Recessions cause readjustments and disruptions in the market's priorities and values. In such times, many companies reassess their supplier lists and look for cheaper options. They seek to reduce costs by outsourcing in-house functions to companies that can perform the same jobs for less. These actions shake up the old order, thus enabling new kids on the block, and even established warhorses, to jump in and take advantage of new openings not available in between recessions.

As most companies pull in their horns and hoard their cash, recessions provide unique opportunities to launch new marketing programs from existing products, and even launch new products. Like hurricanes downing all the trees in their path, *recessions level the playing field*. Any company, regardless how small, now has the opportunity to plant a new "tree," be it by starting a new aggressive promotional program, by introducing a new feature to an existing product, or by launching a new product altogether.

A Bain study mentioned on their Web site, www.bain.com, found that more than a fifth of companies in the bottom quartile in their industries jumped to the top quartile during the last recession. Meanwhile, more than a fifth of all leadership companies – those in the top quartile of financial performance in their industry – fell to the bottom quartile. Only half as many companies made such dramatic gains or losses over a period of time of similar duration before or after the recession.

EXAMPLE Competitive Racing

A parallel can be drawn from competitive sports. Strong runners and bicycle racers often choose times of stress to mount attacks. They increase their pace during rain, on steep hills, or under other challenging conditions, leaving other competitors in their tracks.

FACT 3 Recessions *weaken the competition.*

Many competitors are shell-shocked when recession hits: their good-times-oriented marketing is in disarray, their creativity is brought to a standstill, and conventional thinking is encouraged among the rank and file. Most everyone acts like deer frozen in the headlights.

Competitors are also weakened by a shortage of investment capital and become short staffed due to cost-saving layoffs. During recessions, customers demand perfection for their stingily spent cash. As a result, the already-short-staffed customer service gets overwhelmed by customer queries, complaints, and requests for exchanges and refunds.

FACT 4 Recessions make it *easier to plan ahead.*

In a nonrecession environment, planning is difficult due to ever-changing market conditions. Typically, as you are planning your next business move, things around you change, and you have to revise your plans because customers and competitors are continuously moving targets. They don't stand still waiting for you; they are acting on with their own agendas. *Recessions slow down these changes.* Customers and competitors become more fixed in their positions, thus making it much easier for you to plan.

During recessions, customers stick with the basics: lower prices, better value, surer bets, and less risky decisions. Competitors also go back to basics: they minimize investments in new plant and machinery, they have fewer product launches, and there are fewer marketing initiatives.

FACT 5 Suppliers are *more accommodating* **during recessions.**

Buying raw materials, components, machinery, products, and services becomes easier during recessions. Suppliers fight for every piece of business so they'll do things for you that they wouldn't think of doing in good times. They're more flexible with their payment terms, they offer lower prices, and they make an effort to deliver better products and services. They'll offer direct drop shipping and free shipping. They'll throw in freebies and volume discounts. They'll offer free installation and extend their warranties. Quite often, all you have to do to take advantage of these terms is ask.

FACT 6 Strategic partnerships are easier to establish during recessions.

During nonrecession times, strategic partnering is difficult as everyone is busily serving their customers and generally wants to do their own thing, forging ahead with fulfilling their own dreams and aspirations. Recessions change that mind-set. Potential partners now have more time for meetings, independence does not seem that important anymore, and they impose fewer deal constraints.

During recessions, businesses seek to reduce costs and risks by partnering up with other companies. They are open to have other companies manufacture, distribute, and retail for them. They are willing to replace in-house sales departments with outside sales reps. They are more open to sending their software development and customer service operations offshore. They may even consider having other companies do their research and development.

FACT 7 Employees are *more productive* during recessions.

During recessionary times, employees become more productive due to several factors:

   A. They are fearful of losing their jobs.

   B. They are fearful of being reassigned.

   C. They become more flexible as to the types of work they are willing to take on.

   D. They are willing to work longer hours.

   E. They become more compliant to company policies.

   F. They become less demanding regarding working conditions.

Unfortunately, as you will see later on in this book, employee productivity could also be pushed the other way by the emotional toll extracted by unrelenting fear.

FACT 8 Talent becomes *more readily available* during recessions.

Good people you could never reach before become available during recessions. Many are either laid off, interested in getting more stable employment, or want to change careers. As things slow down at work, people have more time to think and reevaluate their jobs and their lives. They will answer your calls and more freely talk to you about your job offer. They will take off from work and meet you even if it is far away. They will go the extra mile they wouldn't during good times.

FACT 9 Customers are *more easily persuaded to switch suppliers* during recessions.

During recessions, customers will buy everyday commodity products from any trustworthy supplier that can offer a better price. Long-term supplier loyalties are weakened, thus bonds and relationships with existing suppliers can be broken more easily. Survival is the word of the day, and customers feel justified to do whatever is in their best interest to help them survive the recession.

FACT 10 Recessions are *good times to launch* new companies and new products.

History shows that *recessions are good times to launch new companies and new products.* During recessions, most everything you need to start a new company can be gotten cheaper. You can get a better deal on leasing office, plant, and warehouse space. Most raw materials cost less. Advertising is cheaper. Prices, selection, and financing costs for just about anything are better. There are fewer construction bottlenecks: materials are available when and as you need them, subcontractors are more flexible on schedules and costs, building inspectors are not overtaxed, and building departments get right to your application.

Here are some startling facts: *many great brands were born during recessions*, and no fewer than twenty-five of the thirty companies making up the Dow Jones stock index were started during or immediately after recessionary times (see appendix 1).

The following are some well-known companies and products launched during recessions and a short story for each one of them describing the circumstances of their "birth":

1873

General Electric

Henry Villard was a journalist-turned-financier born in Germany to a prominent family. In 1853, after a disagreement with his father, he immigrated without his parents' knowledge to the United States. He first made his living as a journalist, but during the Panic of 1873, he turned to railroad financing and, together with Thomas Edison, the famous inventor of the electric bulb, eventually merged smaller companies to form the Edison General Electric, the forebear to General Electric.

1923–1924

Disney

Walt Disney came to California from Kansas in the summer of 1923 in the middle of a deep recession, with dreams and determination, but little else. He soon got a contract to produce a cartoon series and formed the Disney Brothers Cartoon Studio together with his brother Roy. Later named The Walt Disney Company, it has become one of the biggest Hollywood studios and owner and licensor of eleven theme parks and several television networks, including ABC and ESPN.

1929

BusinessWeek **Magazine**

The *BusinessWeek* magazine, as it was originally called, was launched by publisher McGraw-Hill soon after the start of the 1929 depression to take advantage of the public's voracious appetite for in-depth financial news.

Fortune **Magazine**

Fortune magazine was founded by *Time* founder Henry Luce in February 1930, four months after the Wall Street Crash of 1929 that marked the outset of the Great Depression. He felt the market needed a publication that addressed the grave economic situation with depth of understanding and social conscience.

Hewlett-Packard (HP)

Bill Hewlett and Dave Packard graduated in electrical engineering from Stanford University. The company originated in a garage in Palo Alto during a fellowship they had with a past professor, Frederick Terman, at Stanford during the Great Depression. In 2007, HP had U.S. revenues of $104 billion, making it the largest technology company in the world.

1957–1958

Trader Joe's

The company began in 1958 as a Los Angeles area chain of convenience stores under the name of Pronto Market. It changed its name to Trader Joe's in 1966. Sales for 2007 were $6.5 billion, ranking it among the top retailers in the United States. The October 2006 issue of *Consumer Reports* ranked Trader Joe's as the second best supermarket chain in the nation.

1974–1975

Microsoft

Following the launch by MITS of the Altair 8800 microcomputer, Bill Gates got MITS to distribute software he developed for the Altair while a student at Harvard University. Gates left Harvard University, founded Microsoft, and moved to Albuquerque, New Mexico, where MITS was headquartered. In 1979, the company moved from Albuquerque to Bellevue, Washington, which is still its home today. Microsoft dominates the software market, but also makes the Xbox line of gaming products and a number of computing and gaming products, including mice, keyboards, joysticks, and gamepads. There have been tens of books written about Gates and Microsoft. The world is fascinated by the company's amazing success story and the fact that Bill Gates is now one of the richest men in the world.

Super 8 Motels

Ron Rivett and Dennis Brown opened the first Super 8 motel in Aberdeen, South Dakota, in 1974. They set the room rate at a recession-friendly $8.88 per night. The company expanded quickly and cheaply through franchising. To bolster its image as the low-cost competitor to established brands, it located its motels as close to Holiday Inns as possible.

1981–1982

Airline loyalty programs

The airline industry's first frequent-flier program, the AAdvantage travel awards program from American Airlines, was quietly rolled out in early 1981, with 283,000 members who accumulated points for the miles travelled, which they could exchange for free tickets. Eventually, every major airline adopted a similar plan, and today over 75 million people worldwide belong to at least one frequent-flier program.

IBM Personal Computer

In August 1981, IBM, then the largest and most respected computer company in the world, released the IBM PC. The *PC* stood for *personal computer*. The computer cost around $1,500 (about $4,000 in today's dollars), which was several times less than the cheapest computer available from IBM at the time. Businesses and the public took to it immediately, and tens of thousands were sold in the first year. Four months after IBM introduced the PC, *Time* magazine named the computer "Man of the Year."

CNN

CNN (Cable News Network) was founded in 1980 and is currently owned by Time Warner. It was the first operator to provide twenty-four-hour television news coverage, and it now rates as America's number one cable news network. By 2008, CNN was available in almost 100 million U.S. households and to more than 1.5 billion people in over most countries around the world.

Indoor tanning salons

The $5 billion indoor tanning industry provides tans to 30 million people every year. The industry was born during the recession of the early 1980s, when the prime interest rate was 20%, gas prices were very high due to the Iranian oil embargo, unemployment was high, and consumer confidence was low. People wanted to go to the beach to get a tan but couldn't afford it. Tanning salons conveniently brought the beach sun to their neighborhoods.

Sun Microsystems

Sun's workstations enabled buyers to lower costs and boost efficiency at a time when cost cutting and increased efficiencies were imperative during the early-1980's recession.

Compaq Computer

The name "Compaq" was derived from "Compatibility and Quality." Compaq produced some of the first computers that were compatible with the dominant brand at the time, the IBM PC, but sold for less money.

2000–2001

Crest Whitestrips

Crest Whitestrips is a tooth-whitening product introduced in 2001 by Procter & Gamble as an affordable alternative to the expensive procedures performed by dentists. It is now used worldwide in over 14 million homes.

Apple iPod

The iPod's development began at the time of the dot-com bust. It was developed in just one year and was launched by Apple in October 2001, at a time when most other technology companies were pulling in their horns. Over 175 million iPods have been sold to date, which makes the iPod the fastest-selling music player in history. The iPod has transformed how tens and tens of millions of music lovers acquire, manage, and listen to music.

✿ ✿ ✿

CHAPTER 4
Business Warfare

The object of fighting is the destruction or defeat of the enemy.
– General Carl von Clausewitz (1780–1831), Prussian soldier, military historian, and influential military theorist

Introduction

Much has been written about the similarities between business competition and military wars. Using war as the paradigm is the simplest way to develop business strategies. Since SWIPPE™ is a recession-battling system operating during the warlike environment of recessions, it is important to understand a few of the basics of war.

✯ ✯ ✯

FACT 1 Humans are born with a *need to win*.

Most of us want to win. It's in our DNA, left there from a time thousands of years ago, when we fought wild animals and other human hunters for our meals. When we didn't win, we didn't eat. Not winning time and time again meant death. Those of us alive today are direct descendants of the fighters that survived the years and years of battles. We survived long enough to procreate and long enough to protect our children until they were able to hunt themselves. We still hunt and crave to win today; only the hunt is different now as few of us hunt to eat. Modern society has replaced the old hunt with gambling, sports contests, business competition, competing for jobs, and bringing home a paycheck.

Our drive to win manifests itself as early as the playground when Billy says, "I can get to the top of the jungle gym climber before you." You feel the immediate urge to climb to the top first, but Billy got a jump start on you. He's already climbing, and all you can do is watch his behind as he scoots up the steps, higher and higher and higher. You hope he won't make it, but he does, and now you feel bad. So you make yourself feel better by making excuses: "That wasn't fair." "Anybody can do that." "I could do it if I wanted to, but I didn't." No matter what, you still feel bad. You're not at the top. Billy won. You lost. Even if you got to the top now, the best you could do is be second. Not first, because Billy already did that. Forever and ever, Billy can boast, "I got to the top before you."

FACT 2 There are *very few popular books on war.*

Many books have been written on the topic of war. While most of them are read only by military historians and strategists, two of these books have become very popular with nonmilitary readers: *On War* by Carl von Clausewitz and *The Art of War* by Sun Tzu. These two books have inspired countless other writers who have attempted to apply their teachings to a variety of areas, including business.

On War and *The Art of War* are so central to the Western world's understanding of war that there have been thousands upon thousands of books written *about* these books, their authors, and their teachings. There are no fewer than 8,282 books on Clausewitz and 6,565 on Sun Tzu listed for sale on Amazon.com (as of April 2009). It is difficult to decide which of these books are best for understanding Clausewitz and Sun Tzu and their theories of war, let alone how these teachings apply to business in general and recessions in specific. Through the years, I have read many of these books and tested many of their teachings in my own strategic positioning practice. Much of my learnings are discussed in subsequent chapters.

One of these learnings is so important that it should be addressed now, before going any farther: having uniquely superior weapons is arguably the most crucial element to winning.

FACT 3 Business is a *relative newcomer* to the world of major competitive battles.

Compared to war, business is a relative newcomer to the world of major competitive battles. In fact, until a couple of hundred years ago, there were very few business organizations large enough to engage in major competition. While business competition in general has been likened to war, recessions raise the bar to a whole new level. Conflicts during recessions are over the two key resources that businesses always need in order to stay alive: *customers* and *financing sources*. During recessions, customers become increasingly cash-strapped. They are tougher to convince to use their dwindling cash to buy products and services, unless they are absolutely necessary. As a result, competitive conflicts over customers escalate with deep price cuts, giveaways, and other forms of purchase incentive.

At the same time, the alternative source of cash for businesses, their investors and lenders, are tightening their own purse strings. You could say that during good times in between recessions, businesses engage in relatively silent competitive wars. During recessions, these silent wars escalate into loud, all-out warfare.

FACT 4 Business competitors must be treated like *enemies*.

I first got introduced to the concept of marketing warfare by Jack Trout. I was fortunate to attend one of Jack's first "Attacking the Competition" seminars in 1978, when he was president of the Trout & Ries advertising agency. Trout and Ries have since become famous for their series of groundbreaking books on marketing warfare and strategic positioning, including the bestsellers *Positioning: The Battle for Your Mind, Marketing Warfare,* and *The 22 Immutable Laws of Marketing: Violate Them at Your Own Risk!*

The most impactful learning for me was this simple fact: *competitors must be treated like war enemies.* Their sales have to be "killed," or they would "kill" yours.

FACT 5 Wars are won by the side with *the most surprising and effective new weapon.*

Warfare has always involved weapons and soldier gear, from spears and chariots to assault rifles and tanks, from submarines to aircraft carriers and from aircraft-dropped bombs to human bombs and dirty bombs. Over the centuries, weapons have always been central to waging wars. What is less known is this crucially important fact:

Most wars have not been won by the side with the best soldiers; rather, they were won by the side with a surprising new and significantly superior weapon.

EXAMPLES Surprising New Weapons

Spear
Let's start with the *spear*. Its introduction shifted the balance of power between warring humanoids thousands of years ago. Those who first had them won hands down over their boulder-throwing enemies, who didn't know how to defend themselves against the sharp spears.

Gunpowder
Imagine their opponents' surprise when the Chinese introduced *gunpowder*. It was first put to use against Mongol invaders at the battle of Kai-Keng in 1232. Outmatched in number, the Chinese still handily defeated the Mongols physically and psychologically with their amazing "fire arrows," against which the Mongols didn't know how to defend themselves.

Crossbow
The *crossbow* was a favorite among Middle Age armies. New and surprising innovations to the crossbow by the Third and Fourth Crusades made it a major player in the victories won by the European side and were decisive in conquering Constantinople.

Machine Gun

Unveiled in 1885, the Maxim was the first *machine gun* that delivered reliable firepower. It could fire five hundred rounds of ammunition per minute and seldom broke down when properly maintained. The British used it extensively during their successful colonial expansion in Africa. During the Matabele Wars, a small group of British soldiers overpowered five thousand Ndebele warriors who didn't stand a chance against the Maxim.

Submarine

Though Germany in the end lost in World War II (1939–1945), its fleet of *submarines* stalked and destroyed Allied convoys in the Atlantic so successfully in the war's first few years that Germany was able to conquer France and many other countries with virtually no opposition.

Radar

The *radar* ultimately gave victory to the Allies in World War II. British and American scientists devised a radar system that was extremely effective detecting U-boats and played the decisive role during the hard-fought battles of the Atlantic.

Atomic Bomb

The *atomic bombs* dropped on Hiroshima and Nagasaki in August of 1945 ended World War II. The atomic bomb also established the United States as the world's new superpower, eclipsing the heretofore-powerful Soviet Union, Britain, Germany, and Japan.

Stealth Aircraft

After the Soviet Union's collapse in 1991, most historians agreed that this incredible event would not have been possible without the United States' *stealth bomber* and *stealth fighter*. These airplanes were developed in great secrecy with stealth characteristics that allow them to penetrate an enemy's most sophisticated defenses unnoticed. They have radar footprints similar to that of a bird, enabling them to successfully evade infrared, sound detectors and the visible eye. During the Gulf War (1990–1991), the stealth fighter had 1,200 sorties, with 0 losses. The United States completely decimated the Iraqi army, the world's fourth largest at the time, in a matter of weeks. Top Soviet generals informed the Soviet leadership that no amount of additional spending would enable them to develop a counterfoil to these new weapons. Once they realized that the dictatorship had no defensive capabilities against potential American liberators, the Soviet people seized the opportunity: they revolted, and the Soviet Union collapsed.

COMBATANTS

CHAPTER 5

Business Warriors

The best way to predict the future is to create it.
– Peter F. Drucker (1909–2005), American writer
and management consultant

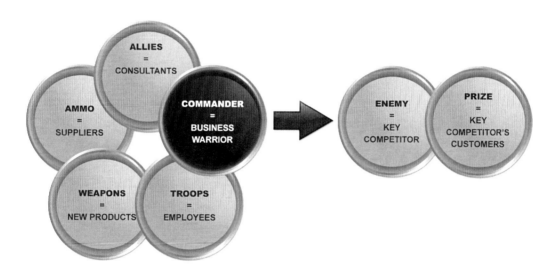

Introduction

This chapter shows what skills and attitudes it takes to be a Business Warrior and describes the key tactics needed to succeed.

✵ ✵ ✵

WARRIOR TACTIC 1 Think of yourself as a *ferocious warrior.*

Business Warriors are entrepreneurs, business owners, and managers who decide to fight recessions rather than give in to them. They end up surviving recessions, thriving in them, and even dominating their markets by the time the recessions are over.

To become Business Warriors, entrepreneurs, business owners, and managers must first change their mind-set from being powerless bystanders to becoming *ferocious warriors.* They must hate their competitors and everything about them: their products, their company name, their product names, their way of doing business, their prices, their advertisements, everything! They must think of their competitors as enemies who want to deprive them of sales and profits. They must start their mind-set transformation process by appreciating two important facts:

FACT 1 All of us can do things now that we could not do at one time.

We can now walk and talk, yet as babies, we couldn't. We can now drive cars while as toddlers, we couldn't. There are also many things that we couldn't do before, and we still can't. For example, most of us cannot score three-pointers from the center of the basketball court, and never could. But if we think long and hard, there are very few average day-to-day things that with a bit of training, we cannot do at least at an *acceptable level.* All tactics outlined in this book fall into this category. Executing them well does not require talent, inborn qualities, or luck. It requires knowledge, and this book imparts that knowledge.

FACT 2 If they don't "kill" the competition, the competition will "kill" them.

Top competitors that dominate markets "shoot to kill" and "don't take prisoners." When you compete with them, if you don't get them first, they will get you. It's that simple.

WARRIOR TACTIC 2 Ignore your chronological age; it's your *mind-set* that counts.

Let's start by putting one big myth aside: it doesn't matter how young or old you are in order to win competitive business battles and be successful in business.

EXAMPLE Kroc, Colonel Sanders, Hitchcock, Cezanne, Gates, Page, Brin

Ray Kroc started the McDonald's hamburger chain at fifty-seven. Colonel Sanders launched Kentucky Fried Chicken at sixty-three. Alfred Hitchcock began making movies in his late fifties. The great painter Cezanne had his first one-man show at fifty-six. All of them survived and prospered through recessions. At the opposite end of the age spectrum, Bill Gates started Microsoft in the middle of the recession of 1975–1976 when his was just twenty years old. Larry Page and Sergey Brin launched Google in the middle of the dot-com crash and the recession of 2000–2001, when they were in their twenties.

✻ ✻ ✻

WARRIOR TACTIC 3 Treat every challenge as a *problem-solving exercise.*

People's behaviors seldom seem rational, and some of these seem downright absurd, especially under the stressful conditions of recessions. These behaviors create most of the challenges we encounter in business. Because of this seeming irrationality, many situations defy intuition; as a result, they require *solving problems* that seem unique and without an easy answer.

Solving problems is *the predominant intellectual skill* required of people in nearly every setting, even outside of business: at home, at school, at work, and at play. Unfortunately, the vast majority of people do not know how to solve problems in a consistent and efficient manner. The root cause for this sorry state of affairs is that *our schools do not teach general problem-solving skills.* They only teach pupils how to solve specific types of math and science problems; they simply do not teach how to solve any other type of problems. As a result, when most of us think of problem solving, we think of solving math and science problems; and since most people feel math and science challenged to one level or another, they assume that they are also *problem-solving challenged*, thereby simply giving up on even trying to become proficient in problem solving.

To be successful, Business Warriors *must* know how to solve problems. We're not talking about math and science problems; there are very few occasions when such problems arise in the typical business setting. We're talking about knowing how to solve shipping problems, merchandising problems, supplier problems, customer problems, personnel problems, manufacturing problems, competition problems, and a myriad of other types of problems that businesses face each and every day.

Because of the importance of solving problems in practically everything we do at every level of our society, problem solving has been researched for years and years by virtually thousands of scientists. As a result, there are now many different problem-solving methods available, some of them very complex, some less so. We have brainstorming methods, brain-writing methods, mind-mapping methods, the NM method, the equivalent transformation method, the KJ method (see example below), and more.

Fortunately, there is relative wide consensus that in general terms, the following is the most efficient process for solving simpler problems such as the ones we deal with in business:

Step 1. List all the *symptoms* of the problem.

In this first step we ask ourselves:

- What makes us think this is a problem?

- How does the problem manifest itself? What are the symptoms?

- What are the root causes of each symptom?

- Who has experienced the same problem?

- How frequently has the problem occurred in the past?

- Under what circumstances does this problem occur?

- How would we describe this problem to an outsider?

- How are people affected?

- What makes this happen?

- What other problems does it cause?

- What are the most damaging aspects of this problem?

- What and who stops us from solving the problem?

Step 2. *Define* the problem.

One of the important findings of decision-making researchers is that well-defined problems are more easily solved than imprecisely defined problems. In my experience, very well-defined problems usually have obvious solutions. This is why spending time and reaching consensus on defining the problem is so critical. Unfortunately, most people gloss over the problem definition and jump to conclusions as to *the* solution. Reaching consensus as to what the problem is by those who (a) will have to eventually implement the solution to the problem, and (b) will have to live with the solution to the problem, is *by far the most important step in problem solving.*

Problems are layered like onions; to get to their core, one must patiently peel off layer after layer.

EXAMPLE Why Were Our Sales Down Last Quarter?

Let's say a meeting was called to deal with the problem of lower sales than expected in the last quarter. Many possible reasons were considered by the group, among them,

A. The customers are not buying as much.

B. The company cannot deliver fast enough.

C. The company's products are defective.

After some deliberation, it was decided that onion layer number 1 can be peeled off: the cause is *A, the customers are not buying as much.*

Next, the group examined why the customers are not buying as much and looked at the following possible causes:

A. Most customers have large unsold inventories of product from the previous quarter;

B. The competition has launched a major sales initiative during the quarter;

C. The company's sales department has become less effective than in previous quarters.

After some more deliberation it was decided that onion layer number 2 can be peeled off: the cause is *B, the competition has launched a major price reduction initiative during the quarter.*

Next, the group worked on figuring out why the competitor's price reduction initiative slowed down the company's sales, and looked at the following possible causes:

A. The company's sales department did not respond to the challenge quickly enough.

B. The prices offered by the competition were too low and couldn't be matched by the company.

Once again, the group deliberated and determined that onion layer number 3 can be peeled off: the cause is *A, the company's sales department did not respond to the challenge quickly enough.*

Next, the group worked on determining why the company's sales department did not respond to the challenge quickly enough, and looked at two alternate answers:

A. The company's sales department was not aware that the competition launched a major sales initiative.

B. The company's sales department knew of the competition's sales initiative but was under the impression that there was nothing they could do to affect the outcome of the competition's sales initiative.

The group deliberated and concluded that onion layer number 4 is *B, the company's sales department knew of the competition's sales initiative but was under the impression that there was nothing they could do to affect the outcome of the competition's sales initiative.*

Now the group tried to determine why the company's sales department was under the impression that there was nothing they could do to affect the outcome of the competition's sales initiative. It came up with two possible answers:

A. The company's sales department was misinformed: the offering attributes (price, product configuration, packaging, etc.) *could* have been changed.

B. The company's sales department was correct: the offering attributes (price, product configuration, packaging, etc.) *could not* have been changed.

Finally, the group peeled back onion layer number 5 and determined that what had happened was *A, the company's sales department was misinformed: the offering attributes (price, product configuration, packaging, etc.) could have been changed.* This then became the consensus as to what the problem definition would be going forward:

The company's sales department was misinformed: the offering attributes (price, product configuration, packaging, etc.) could have been changed in response to the competitor's price reduction initiative, thus enabling the company to potentially neutralize the competitor's initiative's effect on the company's sales, and possibly even increase its sales.

Step 3. Generate *alternative solutions* **to the problem.**

There is always more than one solution to any problem, so ask yourself, what could all the possible solutions be? The more possible solutions you can come up with, the more likely you are to find that one *perfect* solution. A good way to come up with creative solutions is to use "green light" brainstorming. This technique is more fully described in chapter 14, tactic 58.

Over the past decades, there have been many attempts to create standardized methodologies for coming up with alternative solutions to problems. The best methodology for coming up with alternative solutions to difficult problems, such as those involving science and technology, is TRIZ®. The three primary teachings of TRIZ® are as follows:

1. Problems and solutions are repeated across industries and sciences. The classification of the contradictions in each problem predicts the creative solutions to that problem.

2. Patterns of technical evolution are repeated across industries and sciences.

3. Creative innovations use scientific effects outside the field where they were developed.

Much of the practice of TRIZ® consists of learning these repeating patterns of problems-solutions, patterns of technical evolution, and methods of using scientific effects, and then applying the general TRIZ® patterns to the specific situation that confronts the developer.

Step 4. Choose the *best solution* **from among the alternatives.**

A major pitfall when choosing among alternatives is that those who suggested them become their vocal advocates, sometimes drowning out the other voices. To avoid this problem, use objective comparison techniques, such as the one used in the memorabilia card example in chapter 11. Spend time debating and reaching a consensus as to what factors to use in making the selection *before* starting the process of making the selection itself.

Step 5. *Implement* **the chosen solution to the problem.**

As with everything else in life, "the devil is in the details," as the great painter Michelangelo so aptly said in the sixteenth century. While not much fun for most people, developing implementation plans and tracking tasks to completion is crucial to the success of competitive battles, especially during stressful times such as recessions.

Step 6. *Evaluate* **the after-action results.**

It is important to evaluate the results of every major decision so that lessons can be drawn from successes and failures alike. The military uses After Action Reports (AAR) for this very purpose. The AAR enables soldiers to learn what happened, why it happened, how to build on strengths, and how to improve on weaknesses. In a business setting, AAR reviews should be attended by all the participants in the decision-making process and in the decision's implementation.

The learnings listed in AAR analyses must be as follows:

- Specific

- Thorough

- To the point

- Action oriented

- Not critical of anyone

☆ ☆ ☆

WARRIOR TACTIC 4 Use only *reliable* information to make your decisions.

Carrying out each of the six steps of the decision-making process requires having *reliable information.* This is very important because *most business mistakes are caused by making decisions based on bad information.* Most importantly, Business Warriors must avoid using unreliable information sources, including the following:

- Conventional wisdom
- Hearsay
- Heroic-success stories
- Ideology
- Imitation
- Management fads
- Sales pitches
- Self-appointed gurus
- Urban myths
- What has *worked before*

There is a growing trend to using *evidence-based decision making* in businesses and nonprofit institutions. Evidence-based decision-making requires the following:

1. Facing the hard facts
2. Building a culture of telling the truth even if unpleasant
3. Doing what it takes to get the best evidence
4. Rejecting untested facts and beliefs

Since 1999, I have been collecting the URLs of Web sites whose content I feel is reliable enough to be used in evidence-based decision making. There are over twenty thousand Web sites collected to date; they are indexed for easy access and can be utilized for free at www.wordpick.com.

EXAMPLE The Space Shuttle *Challenger* Disaster

A famous exercise that highlighted a flawed problem-solving process and the use of unreliable information was the investigation of the Space Shuttle *Challenger* disaster. In his bestseller *What Do You Care What Other People Think?*, author Richard Feynman, a Nobel Prize winner in physics and one of the most celebrated American scientists of all time, concluded that *"for whatever purpose, be it for internal or external consumption, the management of NASA exaggerates the reliability of its product, to the point of fantasy."* He also said that *"reality must take precedence over public relations, for nature cannot be fooled."*

By using the problem-solving techniques above and ignoring the public relations BS he was being fed by NASA and the unreliable information provided by the manufacturers of the flawed components at the root of the disaster, Feynman was able to show conclusively how the disaster happened and what caused it.

✡ ✡ ✡

WARRIOR TACTIC 5 Use *desperation* to help you "never give up."

The term "warrior" brings to mind thoughts of courage, bravery, selflessness, never accepting defeat, and executing missions with ferocity. The U.S. Army has summed up what it means to be a warrior in its Warrior Ethos, which every member of the army is very familiar with:

1. I will always place the mission first.
2. I will never accept defeat.
3. I will never quit.
4. I will never leave a fallen comrade.

Of all the words of wisdom given to budding entrepreneurs starting up in business, probably the most often used are "Never give up!" The reason is that over and over entrepreneurs appear to have succeeded by sheer determination, staying in the game long enough to see all barriers fall and their goals accomplished.

Unfortunately, nobody seems to agree as to what it takes to make someone never give up. A good clue as to what that might be is to take a look at the circumstances leading to the need to never give up. As it turns out, virtually every case of never giving up I have experienced myself, heard of, or read about points to one pre-existing condition that always seems to be present – *desperation!* Other than obsessed inventors and creative artists, there have been virtually no cases where a businessperson has persevered over long periods of time at great discomfort and risk to themselves in order to accomplish a major objective *without desperation being a major factor.*

The Medal of Honor is the highest award for valor in action against an enemy force, which can be bestowed upon an individual serving in the armed services of the United States. In reading many of the bios of those valiant U.S. Medal of Honor recipients whose heroic acts fell into the category of never giving up, I found that every one of them committed their act of heroism *in desperate situations*: had they not acted heroically, they and their comrades would have met certain death.

As the saying goes, "Desperate times call for desperate measures." An obvious technique for Business Warriors to use in order to assure themselves to sticking with the battle plan until the ultimate win is to *deliberately and courageously place themselves in a desperate do-or-die situation.*

EXAMPLE Forced Desperation

A trick many top salesmen use in order to prepare themselves for success in landing a major account is to go out and buy the most expensive car they can get on credit terms, which they can only afford if they win the account. If they fail to make the sale, then the car would most likely get repossessed, thus disappointing their spouses and children and embarrassing them in front of their friends and neighbors. Talk about pressure!

EXAMPLE Desperate Heroism Leads to Medal of Honor

This is the story of Henry "Red" Erwin, who earned the Medal of Honor during World War II. On Erwin's eighteenth mission, the squadron was assigned to bomb a Japanese chemical plant north of Tokyo, and Erwin's B-29 was tasked to be the lead bomber. At the rendezvous point, it was Erwin's job to jettison phosphorous smoke bombs through a tube in the fuselage of the B-29 as the signal for the other planes to form up.

For reasons unknown, a smoke bomb malfunctioned and exploded in the tube, then shot back into the plane, striking Erwin in the face. Phosphorous at 1,300 degrees began to burn Erwin, blinding him, burning off his hair, most of his right ear, part of his nose, and large patches of skin. In addition to Erwin's wounds, the plane and crew were in mortal danger. Flaming phosphorous was burning through the metal bulkhead. It was now just a question of whether the flight crew would crash into the ocean and explode, or it would explode in midair once the fire reached the bomb bay. In desperation, Erwin snatched up the flaming canister and began to work his way forward, pausing painfully to unhook the latch on the navigator's table, holding the burning bomb between his bare arm and his ribcage to do so. In the process, the white-hot "phosphorous burned through his flesh to the bone," according to an air force report. Erwin worked his way forward and threw the phosphorous bomb out the copilot's window. The pilot jettisoned the bomb load and turned for Iwo Jima for an emergency landing as the crew worked to comfort and stabilize Erwin, who they knew was dying before their eyes.

Red Erwin was awarded the Medal of Honor by General Curtis LeMay on April 19, 1945. Discharged in 1947, Red Erwin underwent forty-one surgeries to restore his eyesight and the use of one arm.

EXAMPLE FedEx Founder Fred Smith and His Desperate Gamble

FedEx had immense difficulties procuring financing for its first official flight in 1973 and did not become profitable until 1976. Fred Smith served with distinction in Vietnam before he put into operation the delivery company he conceived at Yale in 1970. Fred Smith's story is one of perseverance and never giving up no matter what the obstacles.

What is less known is that Smith's struggles were often motivated by desperate fights to stave off bankruptcy. At one time, he was accused of forging papers to save FedEx from impending bankruptcy; later, he was acquitted on criminal charges of bank fraud. On another occasion, out of sheer desperation, he took the last money the company had and gambled it in Las Vegas, hoping to win big and save the company from bankruptcy. He won, and the rest is history. FedEx now operates the largest fleet of civilian aircraft in the world, and it carries more freight than any other airline.

✼ ✼ ✼

WARRIOR TACTIC 6 Change your dictionary and get a *positive mental attitude.*

Through recessionary times, Business Warriors must continuously keep their eyes on the victory to come. They must be able to get their employees out of their funk and challenge them to do things faster, smarter, better. They must be able to challenge their sales force to go for the long shot, those big accounts they wouldn't dream of calling on during good times. They must get everyone on their team to push, think, strive, and move forward. They cannot let them feel sorry for themselves or worry about what might, could, or should happen.

To do this requires that the Business Warriors themselves maintain a positive mental attitude at all times. They must fight the urge to entertain thoughts of failure in spite of all the bad news and depressing talk around them. They must remain confident that they can and they will wrestle recessions to the ground. They must suspend their negativity and disbelief and start using the SWIPPE™ system.

A simple start on the road to recovering from negativity and entering the world of *positivity* is to make a small adjustment to your personal dictionary: trading your noncommittal words with one of the most powerful words in the English language – "will":

Trade	For
Could	Will
If	Will
Maybe	Will
Might	Will
Possibly	Will
Should	Will
Would	Will

Start today and you will be amazed at the results!

EXAMPLE W. Clement Stone, Father of the Positive Mental Attitude Movement

Stone started Combined Insurance Company of America in 1919, and by 1930, he had over one thousand agents selling insurance for him across the United States. By 1979, Stone's insurance company exceeded $1 billion in assets. Motivational pioneer Napoleon Hill and W. Clement Stone teamed up to form one of the most remarkable partnerships of all time. The result was *Success Through a Positive Mental Attitude,* a book phenomenon that proposed to the world that with the right attitude, anyone can achieve his or her dreams. The simple theory of this book is that everyone's mind has a secret invisible talisman. On one side is emblazoned the letters PMA (positive mental attitude), and on the other the letters NMA (negative mental attitude). A positive attitude will naturally attract the good and the beautiful. The negative attitude will rob you of all that makes life worth living. Stone was the greatest practitioner of his own philosophy. He spent most of his life teaching it, preaching it, and amassing a great fortune, most of which he donated to worthy causes such as the Boys & Girls Clubs of America, college scholarships for the underprivileged, the Interlochen Center for the Arts, the University of Illinois, and GROW. Stone lived to be one hundred years old and passed away in 2002.

EXAMPLE Amway's DeVos's Ten Powerful Phrases

Rich DeVos is the cofounder of Amway and chairman of the NBA's Orlando Magic. He is eighty-two years old (2009), the 249th richest person in the world, with a net worth of over $3 billion, and a heart transplant recipient. In his book *Ten Powerful Phrases for Positive People,* he lists the following phrases:

"I'm wrong."

"I'm sorry."

"You can do it."

"I believe in you."

"I'm proud of you."

"Thank you."

"I need you."

"I trust you."

"I respect you."

"I love you."

Enough said.

☆ ☆ ☆

WARRIOR TACTIC 7 Create and maintain trust.

It is fair to say that "trust" is the single most important word in business. Integrity within any organization can only be built by fostering an atmosphere of trust. Trust is the glue that enables teams to function well. Unfortunately, while most people agree that trust is important, few people actually know how to achieve it and how to maintain it on a consistent basis.

Trust is even more important in Business Warriors' work because it is an *excellent source of sustainable competitive advantage.* It is:

1. **Valuable** – It allows a business to better serve its customers and to improve its performance as a result.

2. **Rare** – Few competitors have the relationship between managers and employees that trust denotes.

3. **Costly to imitate** – Trust is ambiguous and socially complex, thus it is difficult for the competition to understand what trust is and how to establish it in its own business.

4. **Non-substitutable** – Trust is a capability that is difficult for competitors to observe, and capabilities that cannot be observed are hard to imitate.

Here is a short primer on how to create and maintain an atmosphere of trust:

1. Make only commitments you believe *you can meet.*

2. Meet all your commitments *exactly* as promised.

3. *Repair the damage done* by your missed commitments.

Of these three steps, the last one is the trickiest, yet the most important. While in some Eastern cultures, such as Japan, repairing the damage done by missed commitments is virtually mandatory, in Western cultures doing so is very rare. Sad to say, in the U.S. business culture *missing commitments is the rule rather than the exception.* Most people's response after missing commitments falls into one of the following categories:

- **Lame excuse:** "*I tried, but it didn't work out.*"

- **Scapegoating:** *"It's not my fault."*

- **Surprise:** *"What commitment?"*

- **Apology:** *"Sorry!"*

- **Cover-up**: Say nothing, hoping no one will notice the missed commitment.

Healthy business cultures do not tolerate such responses; they encourage everyone to face up to their missed commitments and deal with the repercussions. This style of openness and the honesty were the most striking things I noticed on my first job as a young software engineer with Exxon, and it continues to amaze me to this day when dealing with well-run companies.

Paradoxically, acknowledging missed commitments then fixing the damage done by those missed commitments is *a very powerful way to build trust*! It is not known whether this is because of our innate desire to like people who admit they screwed up, but it works.

A quick way to build trust is to seek an opportunity with a high likelihood of missing a commitment and then, once you have missed the commitment, proceeding to *repair the damage done by your missed commitment in a visibly demonstrative way*. Try it yourself, it really works!

EXAMPLE Missed Lunch Appointment

Say you missed a business lunch appointment. Fixing the damage done by your missed commitment could be delivering any one of the following to your lunch partner's place of business:

- Singing telegram

- Large gift basket

- Gift card for lunch for two at an expensive restaurant

EXAMPLE Trust Falls

Many businesses attempt to improve the level of trust among their rank and file via off-site programs. Some of them include trust-building exercises, such as this one:

1. People pair up.

2. One person turns their back on their partner and closes their eyes.

3. The partner with closed eyes acknowledges they are ready.

4. They keep their feet together and body straight and fall backward until they feel the supporting hands of their partner behind them.

5. Repeat the exercise, only this time, the supporting partner moves a little farther away, and so on until the supporting partner is almost a yard away.

6. Real trust is built and experienced by the person "falling" backward.

☆ ☆ ☆

WARRIOR TACTIC 8 Use *precise* communications.

An important way to build and maintain effectiveness is very clear and precise communications. This is especially important in times of high stress and anxiety such as during recessions, when people are more hurried and sloppier in their written and spoken communications. Here are the most common problems encountered when under pressure:

- **Abbreviating key words**
- **Using long, compound sentences**
- **Not knowing who the originator of a report/document is**

☆ ☆ ☆

WARRIOR TACTIC 9 Meditate to relax and improve your focus.

Harvard Business School and INSEAD, the top European business school, have concluded from research that one of the most effective new business tools for the future is *meditation*. Meditation courses have helped industry leaders learn to reduce stress, maintain focus, and stay inspired, while building inner mastery and enhancing overall creativity. Meditation is a mental discipline that enables its practitioners to get into a deep state of relaxation by turning their attention to a single point of reference, such as a single word, or mantra. Although it is practiced as part of almost all religions, there does not need to be any religious content or connotation when meditating.

There are several easy-to-learn secular (nonreligious) forms of meditation. Typically requiring just ten to twenty minutes of practice twice a day in the privacy of your own home or office regardless of the method used, meditation has proven to be one of the most effective ways to relieve the tensions of modern-day living for a richer, healthier, and more productive life.

Dr. Herbert Benson, a Harvard Medical School researcher, conducted clinical tests on meditators from various disciplines, including Transcendental Meditation and Tibetan Buddhism. Based on the results of these tests, he was able to show that relaxation techniques such as meditation have immense physical benefits, from lowered blood pressure to a reduction in heart disease. In his bestselling book *The Relaxation Response*, he demystifies the mantra meditation used in the Transcendental Meditation program, explaining how anyone can reap its most important advantages with or without the help of a guru.

EXAMPLE Transcendental Mediation and *The Relaxation Response*

I learned Transcendental Meditation™ several years ago. Unlike popular belief, there is no religious aspect to TM, and I thoroughly enjoyed taking the course. I especially enjoyed meeting the very interesting people attending the TM center. Although I do not practice it regularly, I always try to meditate during periods of high stress and before important meetings. It makes a big difference to me in several ways: it improves my ability to focus, it helps me think more clearly, and it even helps me improve my word pronunciation. I have also read

The Relaxation Response, and its process is not as convenient to practice and as effective as TM. However, using its method is much less expensive than TM, more convenient to learn, and much more affordable. While a TM course can cost several hundred dollars and take several weeks to learn, *The Relaxation Response* book can be purchased on Amazon for less than $12 and can be read in just a few hours.

CHAPTER 6

Employees

*The productivity of work is not the responsibility
of the worker but of the manager.*

– Peter F. Drucker (1909–2005), writer and management consultant

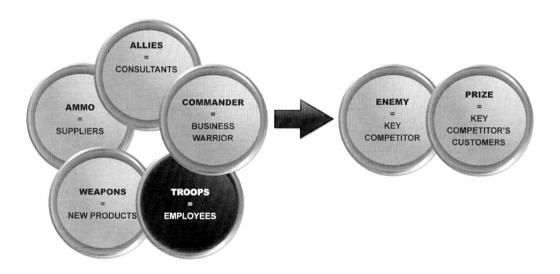

Introduction

In this chapter, we learn the problems and opportunities presented by employees' unique mind-set during recessions. We learn the key tactics Business Warriors must use in order to satisfy employees' emotional needs during recessions, while at the same time helping them to become more productive.

✣ ✣ ✣

WARRIOR TACTIC 10 Help employees fulfill needs *beyond money.*

Studies have shown that while most everyone wants to earn a steady income, we also go to work in order to have a sense of belonging, share the camaraderie of our fellow workers, perform interesting work, get recognition for doing a good job, and be in the know about what's going on in the company. One surprising observation is that the satisfaction of these needs is generally *not within the power of the workers.* Workers cannot create a sense of belonging in their workplace, they cannot easily make fellow workers develop a sense of camaraderie, they cannot give themselves raises, they cannot assign to themselves interesting work, they cannot give themselves recognition for doing a good job, and they cannot easily let themselves in on what's going on in the company. To a great extent, the fulfillment of these wants and needs depends on their managers, the Business Warriors.

Employees are not totally powerless to change their work environment, level of commitment to their job, motivation, and attitude while at work. With proper training and a lot of practice *over long periods of time,* they can affect such changes on their own, and many do. Unfortunately, recessions are not the best time to undertake such personal improvement programs; such programs are best when carried out during non-stress periods. Besides, as most recessions last on the average only about a year and a half and improvement programs can take much longer than that before getting results, the recession could be over before the employees are fully trained.

As most companies have a top-down organizational structure, a much better approach is to make changes by changing the managers' approaches and attitudes toward their employees. There are several tactics in this book that Business Warriors can use in order to motivate employees and help them succeed.

☆ ☆ ☆

WARRIOR TACTIC 11 Help employees choose to *fight.*

For most employees, recessions are dangerous times of high stress and anxiety. Human beings have three ways to respond to danger: fight it, flee from it, or cower in fright. Psychologists refer to this as the fight, flight, or fright response. It goes something like this:

A. We fight the cause of the danger if we feel it is likely we will succeed removing it.

B. We run away if we feel there is little chance of winning the fight.

C. We cower in fear, leaving ourselves to the whims of the threat if we can neither fight nor flee.

Fear has been shown to negatively affect people both emotionally and physically. Many studies have shown that high levels of sustained fear can induce ulcers, high blood pressure, strokes, and heart attacks. Instead of focusing people's minds on doing the best job they can do in order to avoid being laid off, a study by the Center for Work-Life Policy of more than 1,500 high-income U.S. workers has found that uncertainty about job security and increasing pressure to deliver immediate results has the opposite effect: it sends productivity plunging. Levels of stress and anxiety rise sharply, with two-thirds of those polled during the current recession stating that they were not getting enough sleep, up from under half a year before. Of the people interviewed, 24% were actively looking for another job, and 64% were considering leaving their current job. Twice as many women as men were considering leaving, the study found. Key words that kept coming up in the survey conversations included "paralyzed," "demoralized," and "demotivated."

Recessions create a widespread sense of vulnerability in the workplace. They deepen and accelerate trends that have already become noticeable in the American workplace. A recent author has referred to "the psychological recession that's alienating employees and hurting American business." A study of fifty thousand employees at fifty-nine global companies conducted by the Corporate Executive Board determined that *"emotional factors were four times more effective in increasing employee engagement rather than rational ones."* This is most likely why many of the companies listed on *Fortune* magazine's list of most admired companies are also on its list of the most profitable. It appears that there is a direct link between these companies' ability to satisfy their employees' emotional needs and their employees' performance.

Businesses cannot flourish and succeed when their employees are scared and distracted. Fear saps their energy, destroys their trust, undermines teamwork, and dampens creativity. Most importantly, fear robs people of their ability to be themselves, to strive to be better, to succeed. Clearly, then, one of the challenges facing businesses during recessions is to *overcome the emotional burden on their employees.* This is a major responsibility that the Business Warriors must undertake, or face the consequences.

✢ ✢ ✢

WARRIOR TACTIC 12 Answer employees' questions *honestly.*

Among the many questions employees ask during recessions are the following:

- Will the company survive?

- Will I be laid off?

- Will my boss be laid off?

- Will my coworkers be laid off?

- Will I have to work longer hours?

- Will I get a cut in pay?

- Will my tasks change?

- Will my working conditions change?

Business Warriors must be prepared to answer these questions honestly and with great clarity. The best approach is to write down the answers to these and any other questions that may come up and circulate them to all employees.

• • •

WARRIOR TACTIC 13 Deal *decisively* with dysfunctional employee behavior.

High stress such as the one encountered during recessions can trigger certain dysfunctional behaviors such as creating make-work projects in order to ensure increased dependency on themselves, backstabbing coworkers by accusing them of true and imaginary misdeeds, and even sabotaging the work performed by themselves and by others. The productivity of fellow workers can be negatively affected by the dysfunctional behavior of their coworkers. Such dysfunctional behavior must be identified and dealt with promptly by Business Warriors before major damage is done to their businesses. The most important thing for Business Warriors to do is to clarify the responsibilities and accountabilities of every employee. This way, there are fewer misunderstandings among the many that can be created by the dysfunctional behavior of a few.

✲ ✲ ✲

WARRIOR TACTIC 14 *Let go* of the lowest-performing employees.

Low performers use up a disproportionate amount of management time, can upset customers, diminish coworkers' morale, and waste money. Recessions are good opportunities to get rid of low performers with a minimum amount of disruption to the rest of the staff. Coworkers will understand, the business will function more smoothly, and the Business Warrior will have better control of the operations.

EXAMPLE Jack Welch's 10%

Jack Welch, speaking at a technology conference during the recession of 2000–2002, defended the practice he instituted at GE of regularly firing 10% of employees with the lowest performance evaluations. *"It's cruel to keep your worst and then cut them . . . after they've aged, have families, and have fewer choices,"* Welch said.

✲ ✲ ✲

WARRIOR TACTIC 15 Maintain ethical and moral *righteousness.*

Businesses often face difficult ethical dilemmas, such as whether to cut corners on product quality, lay off workers, or reduce portion sizes in order to enhance profits. A current ethical debate concerns the use of extremely-low-wage offshore workers.

In the military, moral righteousness causes soldiers to be in complete accord with their commander, so that they will follow him regardless of the danger to their lives. Thus, moral elements are sometimes more important than wars' material aspects, such as the number of combatants and the weapons they use. Similar to military battles, business battles require ethical and moral righteousness. Employees crave it, customers demand it, and suppliers appreciate it.

EXAMPLE Oprah's Beef

In 1998, Oprah Winfrey, the queen of television talk, was sued for defamation by a group of cattle ranchers from Amarillo, Texas, under a Texas statute that creates legal liability for questioning a perishable food's safety without "sound scientific proof." On April 16, 1996, the price of cattle dropped a dramatic 1.5 cents per pound on the Chicago Mercantile Exchange soon after Oprah's program broadcast that day. At the time, the news media was stridently reporting cases of Mad-Cow disease in Great Britain. During the program, Oprah's guest, a former cattle rancher turned vegetarian, claimed that large numbers of cows that are "fine at night, dead in the morning" get ground and fed to other animals. Oprah appeared to believe that this was unethical and immoral. According to the cattle ranchers who sued Oprah, there was no evidence of Mad-Cow disease in the United States. They claimed that the "Oprah crash" on the Chicago Mercantile Exchange resulted in devastating financial loss for cattle ranchers. During the trial, Oprah stood by her guns and acted on her conscience. She did not back down on her belief that the practices of the beef industry were unethical and immoral. In the end, she was vindicated: she won the lawsuit.

✫ ✫ ✫

WARRIOR TACTIC 16 Manage with *wisdom, sincerity, benevolence, courage,* and *strictness.*

Thousands of books have been written on the topic of how business leaders should treat their employees. Over the past few decades, it has become clear that coercion, manipulation, and other negative approaches do not work well, or at all. While authors and researchers differ over which specific approaches are most effective, there is little dispute that many of the tried and tested approaches used by the military are also applicable in business. Just as the great military strategist Sun Tzu suggested for army leaders, business leaders too must manage using *wisdom, sincerity, benevolence, courage,* and *strictness.*

☆ ☆ ☆

WARRIOR TACTIC 17 Form a *commando strike force.*

Velocity to market is critical to the success of any business. During a recession, the stakes are higher, money and resources are tighter, and time frames are shorter. This "perfect storm" requires leading the battle with people that are experts in their respective areas, tough under pressure, and able to work extremely well as part of a team. To ensure the success of the most critical tasks, Business Warriors should use a handpicked team that can operate like a military commando strike force. Each member of the team must be

- Highly expert in his/her specific area
- Highly reliable
- Totally trustworthy
- Able to get along extremely well with the other strike force members
- Tough and unbending under pressure
- Ready, willing, and able to work 24/7 if necessary
- Able to travel extensively during the term of the engagement
- Totally committed to accomplishing the objectives of the strike force

In addition, the strike force team members must have:

- High energy level

- Excellent health

- Excellent home life

To staff the commando strike force, Business Warriors have four choices:

A. Use *existing employees*

B. Hire *consultants*

C. Hire *new employees*

D. Use a *combination of existing employees, consultants, and new employees*

Given the utmost importance of succeeding with the highly critical missions assigned to them, it is obvious that alternative D is the best way to go when staffing recession strike forces. Tough competitive battles require the best of the best, regardless of where they come from.

To select the best strike force candidates, start by first defining each of the tasks that must be delegated to the strike force, then,

1. Try to find the best people internally. If not available, then

2. Try to find consultants that can carry out the task. If not available or prohibitively expensive, then

3. Hire new employees from the outside, preferably by stealing them from competitors.

✫ ✫ ✫

WARRIOR TACTIC 18 Move the commando strike force *away* from the rest of the operations.

The commando strike force should be headquartered in a place that is physically removed from the rest of the business operations. Such arrangements are typically referred to as "skunk works." Setting up such skunk works is important for several reasons:

A. It insulates the members of the commando strike force from the day-to-day grind, thus enabling them to better focus on their mission.

B. It removes much of the red tape encountered in everyday operations.

C. It insulates the rest of the employees from being distracted by the work of the strike force.

D. And most importantly, it makes it easier to keep the strike force's work secret, thus preserving the mission's element of deception and surprise.

EXAMPLES "Skunk Works"

The skunk works approach is used by leading technology and consumer marketing companies including Microsoft, Apple, Coca-Cola, Procter & Gamble, and Northrop. These groups are given a high degree of autonomy, and they are unhampered by bureaucracy. Most importantly, they have been very successful in bringing to market unique products in rapid time and in great secrecy.

✯ ✯ ✯

CHAPTER 7
Suppliers

Let us ask our suppliers to come and help us to solve our problems.
– W. Edwards Deming (1900–1993), leading quality
production consultant, author, statistician and educator

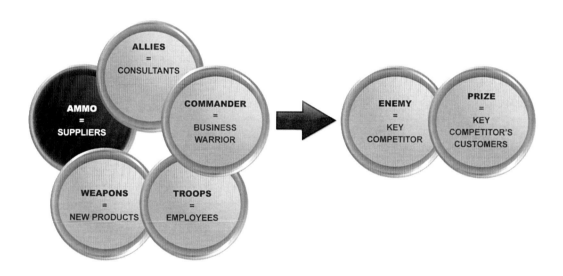

Introduction

In this chapter, we will examine the important role that suppliers play during recessions. Suppliers are to businesses what ammunition is to weapons of war. Just as weapons are useless without ammunition, so is developing and launching new products *impossible without the cooperation of key suppliers.*

✧ ✧ ✧

WARRIOR TACTIC 19 Use suppliers as if they were your *bank*.

At the same time, Business Warriors must remember that in a way, suppliers not only provide products and services, they also provide capital in the form of credit. Without this credit, businesses would have to borrow more money from their banks, a difficult feat during recessions. During recessions, the Business Warriors must take advantage of every single source of cash, and suppliers are a great cash source.

The biggest problem companies have is that unless they are hurting badly, they are not aggressive enough in asking their suppliers for better payment terms and increased lines of credit. This is typically because existing terms were likely negotiated over a long period, with lots of back-and-forth between the managements of the two companies. Purchasing agents and managers that were involved are loath to start the negotiation process all over again. But start it they must, because that was then, and this is now. The recession of today is very different than the good times of yesterday when the terms were originally negotiated. Suppliers know that, and most of them should be prepared to extend additional credit to keep your business.

EXAMPLE Gain an Extra Million

If sales are, say, $1 million a month and a Business Warrior is able to negotiate an extra thirty days to pay the suppliers' invoices, the Business Warrior will have gained *an extra $1 million* to finance his or her business. This is much, much easier than asking the bank to increase the line of credit in the middle of a recession.

✵ ✵ ✵

WARRIOR TACTIC 20 *Resist* supplier attempts to overload you with unneeded product.

Unfortunately, during recessions, suppliers face the same challenges as most other businesses, including falling demand, overcapacity, and downward price pressures. To counterbalance these forces, suppliers push harder to sell you their products. They offer more aggressive discounts and deals, and they try to unload quickly any overstocks and products returned by customers. To understand how severely suppliers will apply pressure for you to buy more, you must know that recessions can reduce demand for many products by 25% and even more. For example, during the recession of 1990–1992, the demand for industrial machinery fell by 24%. As in American football, Business Warriors must play tough defense and offense with their key suppliers. They must counterfoil suppliers' attempts to load them up with products they don't need and can't resell.

✵ ✵ ✵

WARRIOR TACTIC 21 Hold suppliers *strictly accountable* **for performance breaches.**

The nature of business being as fluid as it is, most agreements between businesses have never been honored exactly as their terms require. In my experience, if you look long and hard, you can always find performance breaches that can provide the basis for terminating or modifying supplier agreements. If you decide to take this course of action, make sure you follow a proper process of disengagement: give the proper notices, comply with every one of your own obligations under the contract, and always be respectful and polite with the suppliers' representatives. You will be amazed how many lawsuits have been started because of nothing more than hurt feelings and bruised egos. It would be best to designate the most diplomatic staff member as your point person for such negotiations.

✵ ✵ ✵

WARRIOR TACTIC 22 Build *personal rapport* **with the key suppliers.**

Some suppliers are very critical to a business. There is a good way to get these suppliers to help Business Warriors get through recessions: make them part of new initiatives, be they testing new marketing programs, introducing new features to existing products, or launching new products. During recessions, everyone wants to keep the hope alive, they want to hope things will get better, thus any positive news is most welcome. Business Warriors ask their suppliers for special terms in support of new initiatives. They offer them special mention and co-branding on Web sites and other forms of advertising and ask them in return for longer payment cycles and line-of-credit increases. Business Warriors make critical suppliers a part of the solution before they can become a part of the problem.

During recessions, it is not uncommon for CEOs to get involved in supplier negotiations. This imparts more importance on the proceedings and enables the business to match or exceed the suppliers' ability to bargain.

Building rapport with your key suppliers is crucial if you hope to slow down your payments to them, increase your credit limit, or renegotiate the interest rates charged on overdue payments. Call and tell them you will stand by them and not switch suppliers even as you get calls from desperate sellers. Show them your loyalty, and they'll give you theirs.

✿ ✿ ✿

WARRIOR TACTIC 23 Don't make price the *only* deciding factor.

Negotiating with suppliers during recessions is more intense than usual. Keep in mind, though, that negotiating lower prices is not very useful if the supplier does not deliver on time because he is short of working capital, has payment issues, and delivers poor-quality materials. These are critical considerations during times of recession. Delivery time, payment mode, and additional services are sometimes much more important, as these factors could save significant amounts of money by improving a business's ability to make sales.

✿ ✿ ✿

CHAPTER 8

Consultants

During the Second World War, the Germans took four years to build the Atlantic Wall. On four beaches it held up the Allies for about an hour.

– Stephen Ambrose (1936–2002), American historian and biographer of U.S. presidents Dwight D. Eisenhower and Richard Nixon, professor of history at the University of New Orleans

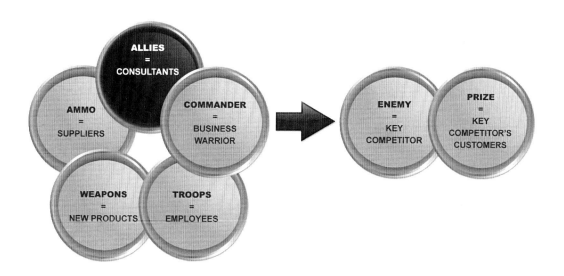

Introduction

In this chapter, we will learn why and how consultants must be used during recessions in order to *provide critical advice on a timely and cost-effective basis.*

✧ ✧ ✧

WARRIOR TACTIC 24 *Be very careful* **when forming alliances.**

Business alliances are appealing, especially during recessions, because they typically do not involve an exchange of money; each party provides their know-how to the other party for free. Unfortunately, business alliances present several problems, including the following:

A. Certain corporate combinations, relationships, and arrangements may be prohibited by anti-trust laws.

B. Company-type allies usually demand much more from the alliance than they are willing to give in return.

C. Confidentiality of information is difficult to maintain between closely allied business companies.

D. It is very difficult to find alliance-worthy companies that have just the right the culture, reputation, skills, and capabilities.

E. Ally companies come with expertise and capabilities but also with "warts": bad reputation, rogue employees, etc., which can seep into your own company's operations.

F. Company-to-company relationships are difficult to disentangle when the alliance is no longer useful.

✻ ✻ ✻

WARRIOR TACTIC 25 Hire *independent* **consultants.**

Hiring independent consultants is an alternate approach to forming alliances. Consultants are free of most of the problems encountered with alliances:

A. There are no antitrust laws affecting company-to-consultant relationships.

B. Consultants generally price their services competitively.

C. Maintaining confidentiality is sacrosanct for all reputable consultants.

D. It is not difficult to find consultants that have just the right culture, reputation, skills, and capabilities.

E. Consultants' warts cannot easily seep into your company's operations.

F. Company-to-consultant relationships are easy to disentangle when the project/alliance is no longer useful.

A lot of times, businesses find themselves needing information and advice not available in-house. This is not surprising, considering our world is so full of choices, complexities, and challenges. Additional reasons to consider hiring consultants are that they

G. Perform tasks that nobody in-house knows how to do as well

A. Perform tasks nobody in-house has time to do

B. Perform tasks that would cost more to do in-house

C. Perform tasks that have a high probability of failure

Most businesses do not hire consultants in the mistaken belief that they are too expensive. Unfortunately, the mistakes made internally by unqualified in-house staff attempting to do critical tasks can be staggering in cost and time lost. I believe *this is the most common reason for business failures* because businesses exist in order to add value to their customers by doing things they cannot do themselves. Incompetence leads to an inability to add such value, thus undermining the rationale for the business's existence.

When it comes to finding the right consultants for the job, there are hundreds of consulting specialties to choose from, including (alphabetically) the following:

- Accounting

- Advertising

- Branding

- Cash management

- Compensation

- Conflict resolution

- Debt collection

- Employee benefits

- Energy

- Engineering

- Environmental

- Facilities design

- Government relations

- Health

- Import/export

- Information technology

- Leadership training

- Legal

- Logistics

- Organizational design

- Packaging design

- Performance appraisals

- Product design

- Quality

- Recruitment

- Research
- Risk management
- Sales
- Search engine optimization
- Security
- Strategic planning
- Tax
- Telecommunications
- Utilities
- Work process design

☆ ☆ ☆

WARRIOR TACTIC 26 Use consultants to *avoid blind spots.*

In her wonderful book *Blind Spots: Why Smart People Do Dumb Things*, Madeleine Van Hecke identifies ten blind spots affecting sound decision making:

1. Not stopping to think
2. What you don't know can hurt you
3. Not noticing
4. Not seeing yourself
5. My-side bias
6. Trapped by categories
7. Jumping to conclusions
8. Fuzzy evidence
9. Missing hidden causes
10. Missing the big picture

Outside independent consultants can help avoid these blind spots, thus enabling Business Warriors to make better decisions. The best consultants are trained to do the following:

1. Stop and think
2. Know what can hurt the business
3. Notice things
4. See the reality
5. Remain unbiased
6. Not be trapped by categories
7. Not jump to conclusions
8. Not decide based on fuzzy evidence
9. Find the hidden causes
10. See the big picture

✼ ✼ ✼

WARRIOR TACTIC 27 Hire consultants who are *most likely to succeed*.

Most people think that intelligence and talent are the most important criteria for predicting success. Based on this belief, they hire consultants based on their academic degrees as surrogates for intelligence. The better the degrees, the more intelligent the consultant is assumed to be. On this basis, Ivy League graduates are more desirable than those from other schools, for example. My experience has been that when it comes to consulting, *demonstrable success in previous significant assignments that were similar in breadth and scope to the contemplated assignment* is much more important than the academic degrees. Unfortunately, most businesses hire consultants with very little background investigation and analysis. The typical consultant is hired based on recommendations from the businesses' accountants, attorneys, or other consultants to the company. The problem with this is that these sources are not themselves experts in the specific consulting discipline they recommend, nor do they usually know the consultants' background well enough to make a sound selection decision.

The better approach is to use the same level of care when hiring consultants as when hiring a top-level executive. Among the areas of investigation should be the following:

- Similar assignments completed to date
- At least three references from businesses for which similar assignments were performed
- Personal background checks, including criminal and civil penalties and judgments

Probably the single most important decision to ensure a project's success is compensation. By far the best approach is incentive compensation directly related to the consultant's contribution to the successful completion of the project.

☆ ☆ ☆

WARRIOR TACTIC 28 *Ensure best legal protection* when hiring consultants.

The following are additional key items to consider when hiring consultants:

1. Have a duly executed written contractual agreement specifying the work to be performed, definition for the terms "completion" and "success," and time frame in which the work needs to be completed.
2. Establish upfront who pays for expenses.
3. Make sure the consultant is available for the assignment as required.
4. Have the consultant sign a letter of confidentiality.
5. Have the consultant sign a letter assigning all intellectual property developed as part of the assignment.

☆ ☆ ☆

CHAPTER 9

Competitors

If you want to make enemies, try to change something.

– Woodrow Wilson (1856–1924), twenty-eighth president
of the United States, president of Princeton University,
governor of New Jersey (1910)

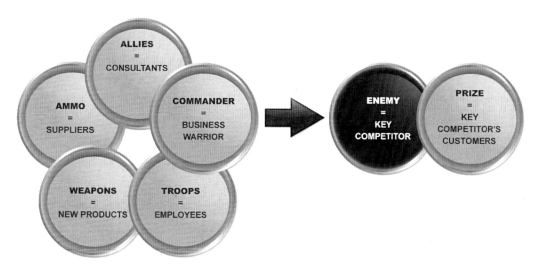

Introduction

This chapter covers the key tactics for dealing with the main nemeses of all businesses: their competitors. Everybody in business worries about competition at one level or another. Yet in my experience, very few businesses worry about competition hard enough. They do not truly appreciate how devastating their competitors are to their business. They don't get the fact that were it not for their competitors, they would have the whole market for themselves. They could then set their prices to the highest level their customers could afford to pay, rather than the lowest needed to beat the competition. Absent the competition, the prices obtained are always higher. At the same demand level, higher prices always mean higher profits.

☆ ☆ ☆

WARRIOR TACTIC 29 Focus on your key competitors, first and foremost.

Most businesses erroneously believe their main objective is to *capture customers by serving them well and giving them the best prices.* In my own experience and that of many successful companies, this is simply *not* enough. What makes a business ultimately successful is this:

Destroying their key competitors' sales.

There are two main reasons for this:

A. Once competitors' sales are destroyed and they are removed from the picture, provided that your product satisfies their needs, their customers will virtually fall into your lap.

B. Their customers are currently buying products fulfilling the same needs as your products, so there is no investment required to teach their customers all of the benefits of your product. You only have to teach them *the additional benefits* to be derived from your product, a much simpler task. Your competition has already done a big portion of the job for you, thank you very much!

The key first step to start the process of destroying the key competitors' sales is to identify *who the most important competitors are.* The military refers to this phase of battle engagement as Identification, Friend or Foe (IFF). Especially in aerial combat, IFF is often the most crucial phase of an engagement. Misreading the cues and failing to identify an enemy quickly is tantamount to signing your own death warrant. There is no in-between in war; everyone on the battle field is either a Friend or a Foe, and the Foes must be killed.

For Business Warriors, there is no in-between either; they must kill or severely wound their competitors' products' sales, else their own product sales will be killed or severely wounded by their competitors. This is why I recommend that as soon as they identify them as foes, Business Warriors start referring to their competitors as *enemies.* This is what competitors are, pure and simple. They must bc called enemies as a reminder to everyone on the Business Warriors' teams that they must be aggressively pursuing the competitors' economic destruction. This is a most important mind-set. Business Warriors must remind their team members of this again and again and again.

✧ ✧ ✧

WARRIOR TACTIC 30 Attack first the key competitors that are *fat, dumb, and happy*.

The majority of today's markets are mature; they are growing very slowly, and they are dominated by a few large companies. Good examples are the energy and food industries. The dominant players are so powerful that they have become complacent. In many respects they have become fat, dumb, and happy (FDH). FDH companies are the best targets for Business Warriors to attack because

- they are slow to react to competitive threats, and

- they have a large piece of the market, so there is a lot of market share available to grab without their being too bothered by it.

✧ ✧ ✧

WARRIOR TACTIC 31 Direct the attacks at key competitor's *center of gravity*.

The competitor's center of gravity (CoG) is the hub of its power and movement on which everything depends. In the military, the CoG includes those characteristics, capabilities, or sources of power from which a military force derives its freedom of action, physical strength, or will to fight. The key business competitor's CoG must be *hit first and foremost*. The old adage *"Hit it where it hurts"* is another way to express this idea. The CoG is often not the competing product itself but its leader, a key employee, a consultant, an ally, or a supplier of a critical component. As the CoG is always linked to the objective of a mission, if the objective changes, the CoG could also change.

It is extremely important to identify and thoroughly understand the CoG of the key competitor and the CoG of a Business Warrior's own business. The

CoG is too important a concept to guess at. According to military planners, and based on my own experience in business, correctly identifying CoGs is the most important task confronting campaign planners.

EXAMPLE Axxess® Attacks Cole National's Center of Gravity and Wins Big

Cole National's namesake and guiding light Joseph E. Cole was born in Cleveland in 1915, the youngest of nine children. He started his retail career with Cleveland's National Key Company in 1935 at the age of twenty. He left National Key nine years later to establish the key division of Curtis Industries, another Cleveland business. Cole's first key shop was set up in the parking lot of a local Sears, Roebuck & Co. store that same year. Joe Cole's key-selling concept was predicated on the idea that key making was a highly specialized, service-oriented business. While mass retailers wanted a share of this segment's high-profit margins, they did not want to deal with the equally high level of training, service, and inventory control it demanded. Cole leased space from such leading department stores as Sears, Roebuck & Co., Montgomery Ward, and Kresge's. He then installed key-making machines, trained store employees to cut keys, and oversaw the operations' complex three-thousand-unit inventory. While it neither manufactured keys nor owned stores, Cole found a profitable niche in providing its services to customers and retailers. Cole would lend them his key-cutting machines with no investment by the retailers, and in exchange, the retailers had to purchase the blank keys from Cole. For many stores, the small key-selling areas emerged as the most productive in terms of profits per square foot.

Unfortunately, there was one problem: the key-cutting machines were difficult to operate correctly, and worse, even when operated by highly skilled operators, they were incapable of cutting keys perfectly each and every time. As a result, as many as 20% of the keys were being miscut. This resulted in a high number of customers returning to the stores and complaining about the product and the service.

In the late 1980s, I was asked by the CreditCard Key Company to help them develop a better strategic direction for the company. The company manufactured patented key cards, plastic cards that have flat plastic keys attached in the middle of the cards, and was marketing to businesses that used these key cards for promotional purposes by placing advertising on the key cards. These key cards are still used as backup keys for homes and cars and can be kept in a wallet just like a credit card.

The first thing I discovered is that the company was suffering enormously from the effects of Cole National's "dirty little secret" – the 20% miscut rate. Many times, the plastic spare keys CreditCard Key's business customers handed out to their own prospects and customers as promotions were miscut by a Cole key-cutting machine. Our customers' customers and prospects would then have to return to the place that cut their keys, only to find they did not have replacement blanks, which, of course, frustrated the retailers. Then the customers would have to contact our customers and ask for a replacement, which bogged down our customers' service staff and eventually our own staff as well.

This triple whammy – dissatisfied customers, frustrated retailers, and our own overworked employees motivated us to find a solution. In the process, we discovered a new business opportunity – the metal keys business – and concluded that Cole National's key-cutting machines was their CoG; it was the key (no pun intended) to their business, and it was vulnerable to attack because of its poor accuracy.

We put together a plan of attack, which included developing a robotic key cutting machine that would cut keys correctly 99.5% of the time, or better. The plan worked: within a few years, the mortally wounded Cole National succumbed to our vastly superior technology and other clever tactics (most of which are described in this book); it sold its key business to us for a fraction of its worth just a few years before, and today Axxess dominates the key market in the United States.

✿ ✿ ✿

WARRIOR TACTIC 32 Attack the weaknesses of key competitors' *leaders*.

Even if they are not the center of gravity of the key competitors, their leaders' weaknesses should be attacked. The leaders may have certain behavioral weaknesses that can provide the opening for the attacks. Some of the most obvious openings are the following:

1. Recklessness

2. Cowardice

3. Bad temper

4. Sensitivity to shame

5. Overcaring for their people

6. Dishonesty

Take advantage of their fault lines by exposing them in interviews, articles, presentations, and conversations with customers and suppliers. Provoke and taunt with the end objective being to defeat them mentally by their own anger, anguish, confusion, and inaction. To avoid defamation claims, always be truthful and give specific examples.

EXAMPLE The Avis "We Try Harder" Campaign

Early on in my career, I started a software company that eventually became the leading provider of auto leasing systems. Among my first clients were both Avis and Hertz Rent-a-Car. Like everyone else, since Avis's "We Try Harder" ads were all about their being the underdog and deserving a chance, I had assumed that Hertz had the largest car fleet. Much to my surprise, I discovered that Avis had, in fact, the largest car fleet, larger than Hertz. Intrigued by this startling discovery, I dug into the history of their rivalry and discovered that the "We Try Harder" ad campaign had a much more devastating effect than reported in the press. Avis had in fact become number 1 but kept it hush-hush lest they lose their position as the underdog! The whole thing started in 1962 when Hertz was the clear leader in the car rental business. At that time, Avis was one of the brands in the pack far behind Hertz.

The Avis "We Try Harder" campaign was launched in 1963; it successfully repositioned Hertz as a big fat cat, and Avis became the right choice in the minds of consumers. Hertz's leaders were incensed by the implication that they were not working hard enough. Too smug and proud to admit they were now number 2 (see weakness 4 – Sensitivity to shame – above), Hertz's leadership decided to intensify their "We're #1" campaign instead, playing right into the hands of Avis. The results were dramatic. In 1962, Avis was an unprofitable company with 11% of the car rental business in the United States. Within a year of launching the campaign, Avis was making a profit; and by 1966, Avis had tripled its market share to 35%.

✻ ✻ ✻

WARRIOR TACTIC 33 Turn competitor's strengths into *weaknesses*.

When no weaknesses are discernible, Business Warriors must find ways to turn competitors' strengths into weaknesses. This is not a physical act; rather, it is something done with words by recasting seemingly good attributes as bad attributes.

EXAMPLE The Avis "We Try Harder" Campaign

The Avis "We Try Harder" campaign (see above example) is also a good example of how to turn a competitor's strength into a weakness. Avis was successful in turning Hertz's strength as number 1 into a weakness by repositioning "number 1" in the mind of the consumer to mean "smug fat cat."

EXAMPLE The "Pepsi Generation" Campaign

Coca-Cola's strength in the soft drink market was that it had long history as the favorite American drink. Pepsi turned Coca-Cola's strength into a weakness with its "Pepsi Generation" campaign, which positioned Pepsi as the drink for the next generation of cola drinkers, the youth market. This positioned Coca-Cola as the drink for the old-fashioned generation. Thus Pepsi turned Coke's reputation as America's traditional drink from a strength to a weakness.

✻ ✻ ✻

CHAPTER 10

Customers

Just because you buy a ticket does not give you the right to abuse our employees.

– Gordon Bethune (1941–), CEO of Continental Airlines (1994–2004)

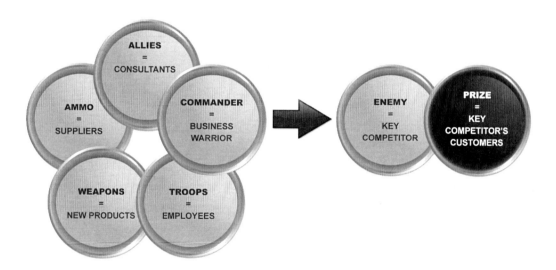

Introduction

This chapter details the tactics needed to conquer the ultimate prize Business Warriors battle for: *their key competitors' customers.* These tactics also apply to the Business Warriors' own customers, who should never be taken for granted; in a free market economy such as in the United States, all customers are accessible to all competitors.

✽ ✽ ✽

WARRIOR TACTIC 34 *Minimize* **the need for customer service.**

There are three types of customer service approaches used in business:

1. Create a unique product in high demand and offer an acceptable level of customer service.

2. Market a run-of-the-mill product of extremely high quality such that it requires minimal customer service.

3. Make a run-of-the-mill product of average quality, and support it with exceptional customer service.

Based on my experience with customer service issues in my own businesses and those of clients, I believe that in times of recession, and even beyond, Business Warriors should favor the first approach above. Instead of using expensive customer service as their weapon to get and keep customers, SWIPPE™ teaches Business Warriors how to accomplish the same objective and more with killer products that solve problems the competition cannot solve. This approach greatly reduces customer service costs while usually improving the customers' satisfaction.

✲ ✲ ✲

WARRIOR TACTIC 35 Get rid of *bad* **customers.**

During recessions, individual consumers and business customers become increasingly demanding of their suppliers. As cash becomes tighter, saving it becomes more and more important, so they scrutinize every bill and every charge. Small problems that would have gone unnoticed before become a big deal. Demands for refunds, exchanges, and rebates increase dramatically. Customer service departments become flooded with real and imaginary problems.

During recessions, formerly good customers can turn bad; stress due to financial setbacks and fear can lead to downright desperation, and they become unfairly demanding, and even abusive. Business Warriors cannot carry on profitable business with too many such customers. The "Customer is king" culture that holds sway during the good times, if left unchecked during recessions, can turn customers into raging bulls. These customers will treat frontline and customer service employees like dirt they trample on. They will be like bulls in a china shop breaking everything around them: employee morale, orderly business processes; and worst of all, they will break the bank. During recessions, Business Warriors must protect themselves and their employees from the effects of bad customers by setting up explicit written rules for dealing with them. When such customers' behavior becomes extreme, Business Warriors must have the courage to stop selling to them before they infect and demoralize their employees with their bad attitude, invectives, and threats.

✵ ✵ ✵

WARRIOR TACTIC 36 Adjust to customers' *changed behavior*.

Consumers' reactions to recessions generally follow well-established patterns. For example, the general trend during nonrecessionary good times is for middle-class consumers to trade up to the luxury trappings of the wealthier classes. During recessions, this same middle class trades down while the wealthy become less conspicuous. Still, during recessions, the wealthy continue to buy what they want, while the middle- and lower middle-class consumers buy only what they need or can afford.

The following are the most common changed behavior patterns that customers exhibit during recessions and how to deal with them (shown in *italics*):

- Reducing purchases of indulgence items such as wine
    Tout the products' ability to reduce stress.
- Holding on to a car a few extra months
    Offer great trade-in incentives.
- Eating out less frequently
    Introduce less pricey takeout and pick-up menus.
- Buying cheaper versions of things
    Introduce cheaper versions of existing products.

- Seeking ways to relieve stress
    Tout the products' ability to reduce stress.
- Using credit cards less
    Offer discounts to cash customers.
- Taking more time to choose and buy durable goods
    Offer great incentives to buy now rather than later.
- Negotiating harder
    Sharpen your pencil to make deals.
- Postponing purchases
    Offer great incentives to buy now rather than later.
- Trading down
    Offer stripped-down versions of your products.
- Buying less
    Offer two-for-one and three-for-two deals.
- Using discount coupons more
    Offer discount coupons.
- Compromising on must-have product features
    Offer stripped-down versions of your products.
- Having less interest in new brands
    Push your well-established legacy brands.
- Seeking affordable entertainment alternatives: beer, liquor, movies, TV
    Give away entertainment tickets as bonus incentives.
- Buying secondhand items
    Open a secondhand department.

EXAMPLE Grunge Music

Grunge music, for example, got its big push during the recession of 1990–1992. Its anger-filled lyrics, stripped-down melodies, the grubby appearance of its musicians and followers, and the rejection of theatrics were embraced by their fans for being reflective of the sparse economic conditions of the time.

✫ ✫ ✫

WARRIOR TACTIC 37 Have *written procedures* for dealing with professional buyers.

Professional buyers that buy goods and services on behalf of businesses are people too, so during recessions, their emotions and attitudes closely parallel those of individual consumers. Although tempered, of course, by their companies' policies, their changing buying patterns during recessions are more dangerous to Business Warriors' financial health because they

A. Buy in larger quantities

B. Have deeper pockets to fight Business Warriors' companies

C. Demand much greater refunds and allowances than individual consumers

The following are a few of the more common behavior patterns of professional business buyers during recessions:

- Reducing purchases of optional items
- Holding on to equipment a few extra months
- Placing orders less frequently
- Buying cheaper versions of the products
- Cutting down their overall purchases
- Making slower payments
- Taking longer to make buying decisions
- Negotiating harder
- Placing smaller orders
- Having less interest in new products
- Willing to buy reconditioned products
- Being secretive
- Being confrontational
- Breaking commitments

Business Warriors must make sure their employees recognize business customers' changing patterns of behavior during recessions and *have predefined procedures in place for dealing with each one of their changed behaviors*. Most importantly, employees must be asked to report each and every negative event involving a professional buyer: complaints, requests for refunds, failure to return phone calls, sudden major changes in buying patterns, etc. If left unattended, such situations can result in significant loss of business and, worse, multimillion dollar lawsuits that could tank the whole company.

✧ ✧ ✧

WARRIOR TACTIC 38 Focus on the customers that can bring in *the most cash.*

Every company has customers that are more profitable than others, and a recession is a time to focus on those customers that can bring in the most cash.

EXAMPLE Singapore Airlines

Singapore Airlines recognized its best customers were business and first-class travelers flying transcontinental routes. So management cut back on short-haul routes, added long-haul routes, and invested $300 million to improve business and first-class service. When East Asia fell into a recession in 1997–1998, Singapore Airlines remained profitable and to this day is more successful than other Asian airlines.

✧ ✧ ✧

WARRIOR TACTIC 39 Carry out *customer satisfaction surveys.*

Business Warriors must carry out customer satisfaction surveys on a regular basis in order to find out if your customers' needs are being met, and if not, what areas need improving. These surveys must also ask customers what their expectations are and how they would describe the "perfect product." Most importantly, the surveys must ask customers how they feel about the key competitors.

Having tried many different approaches for carrying out such surveys, from mall intercept surveys to focus groups, I believe that the most effective method is the online survey. There are a number of Web-based survey services available today that are easy to use and very cost-effective.

EXAMPLE Zoomerang Surveys

One of my clients needed to find out which of a number of new potential products under consideration would be most appealing to their customers. The service provided by Zoomerang at www.zoomerang.com was used to develop a series of questions. Zoomerang invitations to participate in the survey were sent to a randomly selected subset of the customer database. Of the invited customers, 20% responded to the survey, and the data showed a clear preference for one of the proposed new products. Based on this data, the product was developed and launched into the marketplace with great success.

MISSIONS

CHAPTER 11
Mission 1: Find the Top Strength of the Current Product

Only the strong will survive.

– Anonymous

Introduction

The first mission that starts the SWIPPE™ process is determining the strengths of the current product marketed by the Business Warrior. While always important, proving conclusively the product's superiority over the competition is even more important during recessions. This is because during recessions, customers are most careful evaluating the value delivered by products.

✳ ✳ ✳

WARRIOR TACTIC 40 Retrieve product information from its *original designers and marketers.*

Typically, companies know what they are good at and what they are not so good at *as a company*. What they don't know as well is their products' strengths and weaknesses *versus the products' key competitors*. This is because to *really* know a product, you need to understand a lot of facts, some of which can be quite technical in nature and many of which may have been forgotten over time.

There are so many aspects to a product and so many dimensions along which to measure each of these aspects that sometimes only the development engineers that created the product in the first place and the top marketing professionals who launched the product may know and understand them all.

✣ ✣ ✣

WARRIOR TACTIC 41 Compare the current product to the key competitors' products.

In order to determine what the strengths of a Business Warrior's current product are versus its key competing products, an objective analysis of each feature of the current product and its key competitors' products must be carried out. The following is a list of the most important factors considered by professional product developers and top executives when they decide to launch a brand-new product or add new features to an existing product (in alphabetical order):

1. Availability for purchase
2. Benefits to users
3. Convenience in use
4. Cost of supplies
5. Cost to buy
6. Cost to repair
7. Cost to ship
8. Credit purchase possible
9. Customer service cost
10. Customer service representatives
11. Delay payments available
12. Delivery lead time
13. Demonstrability
14. Displayability
15. Durability
16. Emotional impact
17. Environmental impact when discarded
18. Environmental impact when in use
19. Environmental impact when manufactured

20. Aesthetic look wrapped / in the display box
21. Functionality
22. Fragility
23. Installation service
24. Installment purchase
25. Labor used to manufacture
26. Market launch date
27. Ease of learning how to use
28. Look and feel
29. Manufacturing environment protection
30. Manufacturing worker safety
31. Models/versions
32. Obsolescence
33. Options available
34. Ordering ease
35. Patent protection
36. Performance levels
37. Performance vis-à-vis specifications
38. Practicality
39. Reliability
40. Repair on-site service
41. Repairability
42. Safety in use
43. Scalability
44. Size
45. Storability
46. Trade-in value
47. U.S. made vs. foreign made
48. Use ease
49. User interface
50. Value
51. Warranty
52. Weight

✧ ✧ ✧

WARRIOR TACTIC 42 *Strengthen* **the current product.**

If the current product does not have any significant strengths versus its competition, then it must be redesigned to add new features that are stronger. During recessions, three of the factors in the list above become most important to the users, and Business Warriors must try to focus first and foremost on finding product strengths in these areas. If there aren't any, then new features must be added to the product in order to enhance these areas:

1. Durability

2. Practicality

3. Value

I have never failed to find at least one very important area where a product was clearly and demonstrably superior to its competition, or in which a new feature to make it so could not be added. What it takes is a detailed objective analysis of each feature of the product and its key competitor's. The best way to do this is by weighing the importance of each feature and rating how well the feature performs against the competition.

The features that should be added to your list of key strengths are those that have the highest importance to your customers and which also rate the best against your competition.

EXAMPLE The Memorabilia Card

Here is the analysis I used for the Memorabilia Card, a product I have invented and patented. This product is both a trading card and a memorabilia article at the same time. The big differentiator between Memorabilia Cards and regular trading cards is that it contains a piece, but not the whole of an authentic item of memorabilia. The piece could be cut from any memorabilia article such as an authentic game-used jersey or ball used by a famous athlete or from a costume or a prop used in a major movie or TV show.

Key Evaluation Criteria	Importance For The Buyer	Memorabilia Cards		Regular Trading Cards	
Durability	8	10	80	10	80
Practicality	8	10	80	10	80
Value	10	10	100	5	50
Esthetic look	8	10	80	3	24
Emotional impact	10	8	80	3	30
Total points	**280**		**260**		**104**
Score			**93%**		**37%**

In the table above, the column titled "Importance for the Buyer" shows on a scale from 1 to 10 the level of importance the typical buyer ascribes to each of the "Key Evaluation Criteria". A value of "10" means that evaluation criteria is highly important to the buyer and a value of "1" means it is of very little importance to the buyer.

The second column of numbers contains a rating of how well the product rates in the respective Key Evaluation Criteria, with "10" representing the highest rating.

The third column of numbers shows the weighted score of Memorabilia Card in each of the Key Evaluation Criteria, and it is calculated by simply multiplying the Key Evaluation Criteria number with the product rating number shown in the second column of numbers.

As you can see, this is a simple yet powerful way to assess the strengths of your product. In this example, you can readily see that Memorabilia Cards have several advantages over its competition, the regular trading cards. These, in fact, turned out to be the same differential advantages that trading card companies tout in their promotions for Memorabilia Cards. These product strengths have stood the test of time, making Memorabilia Cards the most popular type of trading cards on the market. The ultimate kudos came in 2001 when Memorabilia Cards were voted by experts in the trading card field as the Trading Card Product of the Century. The tactics most important in creating new products are described in later chapters.

✿ ✿ ✿

CHAPTER 12

Mission 2: Find the Worst Weakness of the Key Competing Product

What is bad? All that proceeds from weakness.
– Friedrich Nietzsche (1844–1900),
German philosopher and classical philologist

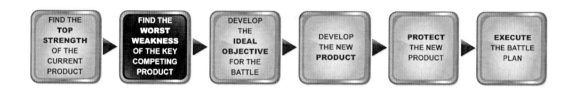

Introduction

In this chapter, we will deal with the next mission in the SWIPPE™ system: finding the worst weakness of a Business Warrior's *key competing product*. These weaknesses are used to *plant Fear, Uncertainty, and Doubt (FUD) in the minds of the enemy's key stakeholders: its employees, investors, allies, consultants, suppliers, and customers.* Business Warriors should undertake this mission *only if the enemies' products absolutely, positively deserve it.* Business Warriors must always take the high ethical and moral road; they must make sure that everything said is in fact *the truth and nothing but the truth.*

✫ ✫ ✫

WARRIOR TACTIC 43 Find *the weakest attribute* of the key competitor's product.

To develop a FUD statement, Business Warriors must start by determining the weakest attribute of the target enemy's product. The list of product features used to determine Business Warriors' own product's strengths can also be used to determine the weaknesses of the enemy product. Here it is once again:

1. Availability for purchase
2. Benefits to users
3. Convenience in use
4. Cost of supplies
5. Cost to buy
6. Cost to repair
7. Cost to ship
8. Credit purchase possible
9. Customer service cost
10. Customer service representatives
11. Delay payments available
12. Delivery lead time
13. Demonstrability
14. Displayability
15. Durability
16. Emotional impact
17. Environmental impact when discarded
18. Environmental impact when in use
19. Environmental impact when manufactured
20. Aesthetic look wrapped / in the display box
21. Functionality
22. Fragility
23. Installation service
24. Installment purchase
25. Labor used to manufacture
26. Market launch date
27. Ease of learning how to use
28. Look and feel
29. Manufacturing environment protection
30. Manufacturing worker safety
31. Models/versions
32. Obsolescence
33. Options available
34. Ordering ease

35. Patent protection
36. Performance levels
37. Performance vis-à-vis specifications
38. Practicality
39. Reliability
40. Repair on site service
41. Repairability
42. Safety in use
43. Scalability
44. Size
45. Storability
46. Trade-in value
47. U.S. made vs. foreign made
48. Use ease
49. User interface
50. Value
51. Warranty
52. Weight

✧ ✧ ✧

WARRIOR TACTIC 44 List the *worst things* that can honestly be said about the key competitor's product.

Once the analysis of its features is completed and you have determined the greatest weaknesses of the enemy's product, create a list of the absolutely worst things that can *honestly* be said about the product. To do this, start by first looking at the following consumption trends of the free economies of the world:

- Overabundance of material goods

- Search for new experiences

- Living in virtual worlds

- Living online

- Expressing individualism

- Participation in meaningful causes

- Feeling guilty for the environment, animals, the poor

- Fame seeking

During recessions, this list can be expanded to include the following:

- Frugality

- Hoarding

- Comparison shopping

Use these broad trends as the focus of the list of the worst things to say about the enemy product.

EXAMPLES

- **Difficult to operate** – *"Nobody can figure out how it really works."*

- **Easy to knock off** – *"Most will buy the counterfeit for a tenth of the price."*

- **Expensive to buy** – *"Nobody can afford it."*

- **Expensive to repair** – *"Nobody will be able to afford repairing it."*

- **False advertising** – *"What they say it does is a lie."*

- **Foreign made** – *"It robs Americans of thousands of jobs."*

- **High energy consumption** – *"It's making us dependent on foreign oil."*

- **Large size** – *"It requires much too much space."*

- **Obsolete** – *"It uses ten-year-old technology."*

- **Poisonous** – *"It can kill children."*

- **Polluting** – *"It can cause birth defects."*

- **Poor performance** – *"It can ruin the job."*

- **Sharp edges** – *"It will cut off fingers."*

- **Small size** – *"It's easy to steal."*

- **Unattractive** – *"It's embarrassing-looking."*

- **Unreliable** – *"It breaks down all the time."*

- **Very heavy** – *"It can kill someone if it falls."*

✯ ✯ ✯

WARRIOR TACTIC 45 Find *fraudulent, life-threatening, and other horrific* **aspects of the key competing product.**

In good times, most businesses look for shortcomings in competing products and try to overcome them with their own products. During recessions, things get much more intense; Business Warriors must turn up the heat and look deeper, much deeper into every single nook and cranny of every feature of the target competing product. They must evaluate the versatility, cost efficiency, ease of use, and effect of the competing products, and they must try to find the most negative aspects of the key competing products. Ideally, these negative aspects are *horrific, fraudulent, and even life-threatening features that end users could instantly feel are totally unacceptable.* I repeat, *totally unacceptable.*

These unacceptable features should be so bad that end users would feel embarrassed to admit they ever bought, used, or even thought of buying or using the competing product. They must be so terrible that when someone is seen using the product, decent folk would be compelled to tell them to *stop using them immediately.* Ideally, these features are so horrific that law enforcement officials and legislators would feel it is their duty to enforce laws and legislate new ones against the manufacturing and selling of the competing product.

✯ ✯ ✯

WARRIOR TACTIC 46 Create the *scariest, but believable, statement* **about the key competitor's product's major weakness.**

Next, the Business Warrior must create one single statement about the key competitor's product's major weakness that is powerful, believable, and defendable. When seen, read, or heard the statement must instantly affect the target audience *emotionally*. It must hook the audience's sense of self-preservation for themselves, their families, and their friends by creating a powerful sense of fear, uncertainty, and doubt (FUD) about the enemy's product. Business Warriors must have trustworthy substantiating evidence to support their FUD statements. Such evidence can be found by searching the Web and articles archived on services such as Lexis.com and HighBeam.com.

The stronger and more powerful the FUD statement is, the more damage will be inflicted upon the competitor, therefore the higher the likelihood he/she will strike back, potentially with a lawsuit. To minimize such occurrences, written opinions should be obtained from an attorney specializing in advertising law and also from an attorney specializing in defamation law.

✧ ✧ ✧

WARRIOR TACTIC 47 Get inspiration for new products from business *disasters and mishaps.*

Because of the complexity of manufacturing and distributing products, there are ample ready-made opportunities to create killer products that address needs created by market disasters and mishaps.

EXAMPLE The Chinese Recalls

Over the past couple of years, we have heard increasingly alarming news about Chinese-made products. From pet food to toothpaste, tires to jewelry, seafood to toys and eggs to milk products, questions have been raised over the reliability of Chinese-made goods. As the death of a child who swallowed a magnet from a Chinese-made toy last year and the illness and deaths of others who have consumed contaminated food suggest, the risks presented by unsafe goods can be great. In Panama, the deaths of some fifty-one people have been blamed on cough syrup tainted with Chinese-made diethylene glycol, commonly used in antifreeze. The same chemical has also been found in toothpastes from China sold in the United States and Canada.

Earlier this year, more than one hundred brands of cat and dog food were pulled from the shelves in the United States after pets died from eating food contaminated with the chemical melamine. Investigators traced the melamine to wheat gluten from China. Such disasters present wonderful opportunities to create new killer products. Just imagine the powerful pitch for a new food product launched to kill a competing product from China:

Save your pets with MelaFree™, the first 100% Melamine-free pet food.

The fine print could read something like this:

Melamine is known to be harmful if swallowed, inhaled, or absorbed through the skin. Chronic exposure may cause cancer or reproductive damage. At the very least, it is an eye, skin, and respiratory irritant. U.S. Food and Drug Administration scientists believe that when melamine and cyanuric acid are absorbed into the bloodstream, they concentrate and interact in the urine-filled renal microtubules, then crystallize and form large numbers of round yellow crystals, which in turn block and damage the renal cells that line the tubes, causing the kidneys to malfunction.

EXAMPLE The International Bad Product Awards

There is a plethora of bad new products launched every year, products that are just waiting to be unmasked and brought to the close scrutiny of buyers. Consumers International, the world federation of consumer organizations, recently announced the winners of the International Bad Product Awards for 2007. The awards aim to highlight failings of corporate responsibility and the abuse of consumer trust by internationally recognized brands. The "winners" for 2007 were the following:

- **Coca-Cola** – For continuing the international marketing of its bottled water, Dasani, despite admitting it comes from the same sources as local tap water.
- **Kellogg's** – For the worldwide use of cartoon-type characters and product tie-ins aimed at children, despite unacceptably high levels of sugar and salt in their food products.
- **Mattel** – For stonewalling U.S. congressional investigations and avoiding overall responsibility for the global recall of 21 million products.
- **Takeda Pharmaceuticals** – That won the overall prize for taking advantage of poor U.S. regulations and advertising sleeping pills to children, despite health warnings about pediatric use.

If illustrious global brands like these can have such glaring cracks in their armor, imagine the rich opportunities for finding flaws in products from lesser companies. Over the thirty or so years I have studied product flaws as part of my strategic positioning practice, I have never failed to find at least one superbad competing product feature, which I was then able to exploit in decimating a competing product. I must admit this type of work has been, and continues to be, most fun. What can be more satisfying than stopping the sale of products endangering people's lives? Or getting counterfeit products off the market and bankrupting the fraudsters? Or getting companies with bogus promises to bug out and stay out of business?

EXAMPLE MotorVac Technologies

One of the companies for which I developed the original strategic positioning is MotorVac Technologies, a company referred to in an earlier chapter of this book when discussing the topic of business intelligence. When I first got involved with this company, it and its competitors saw themselves as being in the business of removing carbon buildup from auto engines. Accordingly, the company was named CarbonClean International. While removing carbon from engines is indeed a much-needed service, most drivers are not aware they have a carbon buildup problem with their car's engine. Thus the resellers of the company's machines had to give lengthy explanations to convince customers to buy the engine-cleanup service. Even worse, as there were a number of other carbon-cleaning products on the market, the company found it difficult to land resellers. By the time I was brought in by the company's auditors during the recession of 1990–1992, the company had gone into Chapter 11.

After carrying out an analysis of the company's product and its competition's products, I determined that its most important differential advantage was a unique patented process: high-pressure vacuum cleaning. Most importantly, this technology made the company's process much more effective than the competition's; it cleaned engines much better than they did. MotorVac's process cleaned over 99.5% of the carbon deposits whereas its competitors' products could do no better than 80%.

To showcase its significant competitive advantage, the vacuum cleaning process it used, I created a new name for the company: MotorVac Technologies Inc. Everyone knows that vacuum cleaning is good, as either themselves or their significant others do it at home on a regular basis. Thus by association, MotorVac Technologies' customers instantly accepted the fact that what's good for their homes – vacuum cleaning – would also be good for their cars. I changed the company's sales pitch to a much simpler, broader, and easier-to-understand mission statement: *"We vacuum-clean car engines."* With this statement, the major flaw of the competitors' products was exposed: they could only clean the carbon, while we could clean everything by sucking it out! Resellers clamored to distribute the MotorVac machines, MotorVac Technologies came out of Chapter 11, and it has since outdistanced most of its competitors. It has become a world leader in engine-cleaning systems.

☆ ☆ ☆

WARRIOR TACTIC 48 Sow *fear, uncertainty, and doubt* about the key competitor's product.

We live in an era of widespread anxiety, from local environmental and financial crises to global political and economic instability. Fear is becoming a driving force for customer behavior, and recessions make matters worse, much worse. It is a powerful attitude changer, especially when it is about losing money, social status, and your job. Sowing Fear, Uncertainty, and Doubt (FUD) is a widely used technique in marketing and political campaigns. This is why this tactic is especially popular in promoting product sales and is at the root of many major cosmetics and health-related product brands.

EXAMPLE Video Game Product Manufacturers

Video game product manufacturers are notorious for using FUD to promote their consoles. In recent years, no lesser lights than Microsoft and Sony have used the FUD approach in the gaming press to attack each other with negative statements about hardware reliability.

EXAMPLE 7 Up as "The Uncola"

In 1968, 7 Up needed to find a defense against Coke and Pepsi, which were both gaining market share. Based on its strategic consultants' advice 7 Up positioned its lemon-lime beverage as "The Uncola." This was a direct attack on Coke and Pepsi, both of which were cola drinks. Since most consumers knew that "cola" implies "caffeine," the clear message was "If you want to avoid the bad effects of caffeine, drink 7 Up." The campaign worked: the first year, sales rose 15%, and ten years later, Philip Morris bought 7 Up for $520 million.

CHAPTER 13

Mission 3: Determine the Ideal Objective for the Battle

The ideals which have lighted me on my way and time after time given me new courage to face life cheerfully have been Truth, Goodness and Beauty. . . . The ordinary objects of human endeavor – property, outward success, luxury – have always seemed to me contemptible.

– Albert Einstein (1879–1955) theoretical physicist

Introduction

Determining what the Ideal Objective should be for the battle is the single most important decision to be made by Business Warriors. In this chapter, we learn what makes a battle objective *ideal* and what tactics Business Warriors must use in order to create an Ideal Objective that *will win the most number of customers away from their key competitors*. Most importantly, this objective will enable Business Warriors to Win With Honor™.

✲ ✲ ✲

WARRIOR TACTIC 49 Use mission statements to *motivate employees.*

Most military units have battle cries. Their purpose is to arouse aggression and bond the unit's members into a cohesive group. From the Middle Ages on, many battle cries appeared on flags and were adopted as mottos, such as the "Dieu et mon droit" ("God and my right") used by Edward III as the rallying cry during the Battle of Crécy.

All branches of the U.S. Armed Forces have battle cries. The U.S. Marines shout "Oo-rah!" and the U.S. Army shouts "Hooah!" The U.S. Navy SEAL teams use "Hoo-yah!" for motivation in training. Because of the tough missions they face, the U.S. Marines understand more than most the need for motivation and bonding. Thus they have extended "Oo-rah!" to mean many more things than a battle cry, all motivational and all bonding. They use it as a greeting and as a response to other marines. For them, "Oo-rah!" has become a mantra to be used around the clock as a reminder of who they are and what they stand for:

1. I am a marine.

2. I enthusiastically accept your order.

3. I am excited to be here.

4. I will do what you ask of me in a manner befitting a marine.

5. I love being a marine.

Similar to the military, business leaders have battle cries too. They typically refer to them as Mission Statements, Vision Statements, and Objectives. These statements are supposed to capture in a few words the business leaders' vision of things to come; they are their picture of the businesses' future. At their best, these mission statements state what the leaders' *ideal objectives* are.

Unfortunately, while they have been used by businesses for many decades now, few business leaders create meaningful mission statements. The mission statements normally seen are watered-down, nonconfrontational statements that sound good but mean nothing and motivate no one. In my experience, most mission statements are a waste of time. They don't create the kind of motivational fervor needed to overcome the heightened negativity experienced during recessions. They do not urge us to Win With Honor™. They do not capture an ideal objective that seems worth pursuing.

EXAMPLE Retailer of Business Furniture

> *To be a provider of quality office furniture, mobile shelving*
> *and a complete line of services enabling us to work as partners*
> *with a wide variety of customers.*

This mission statement starts by saying that this company sells good-quality stuff. Most companies say the same thing. It then goes on to say that the company sells a complete line of services. Many companies I know say the same thing. It continues by saying that this gives them the ability to work as partners with a variety of customers. Why they claim this is not understood, but this is not unusual. Most mission statements make similar "leap-of-faith" statements that have no easy explanation.

Can this mission statement motivate the company's employees to work harder, smarter, faster in order to make the business more successful? No way. Does this mission statement say anything different than what any other business furniture retailer might say? No. So what does it accomplish? Absolutely nothing.

Now let's try the following mission statement for the same business furniture retailer:

> *To help our customers create the safest, most comfortable work*
> *environment for their employees.*

Would this mission statement motivate the furniture company's own employees? Yes, because they are now part of a company that cares in a meaningful way about its customers. Furthermore, they are helping their customers care for employees just like them. They, thus, show solidarity with their brethren. Finally, they now act as safety and comfort consultants, rather than mere furniture peddlers.

EXAMPLE Tire Retailer's Mission Statement

Here is another mission statement found on the Web (the name of the company is changed):

> *The mission of Petersen Tire is to serve our customers and community more effectively than anyone else can serve them. We strive to provide the friendliest and most efficient service possible, putting our customers first before anything else and recognizing that our company must merit and earn the respect and loyalty of our customers.*

While this may seem like an improvement over the previous mission statement, it is not. By this statement, Petersen Tire's employees are told that they must

1. Work more effectively than anyone else

2. Provide the friendliest service

3. Provide the most efficient service

4. Put the customers first before anything else

5. Recognize that the company must merit and earn the respect and loyalty of its customers

As you can see, there is nothing in the mission statement that *moves the employees* emotionally in a positive way. There is nothing *lofty and uplifting*. The only thing that jumps at them is that they must do work, work, and more work.

Now let's make up a new mission statement for Petersen Tire that is emotional and uplifting for the employees, while answering the customers' biggest concerns when buying tires:

> *Our mission is to protect our customers' lives, maximize their driving enjoyment, and give them the best prices anywhere.*

✻ ✻ ✻

WARRIOR TACTIC 50 Shift in your mind what you *believe you can do.*

One of the problems encountered when we try to develop lofty, uplifting mission statements is *negativity*. A great way to resist the negativity of "couldn'tness" is to shift in our minds what we *can* do. The easiest way to do this is to follow a short yet powerful slogan that empowers and uplifts us. Having just witnessed the rapid ascension of Barack Obama, the former junior senator from Illinois, to the highest office in the nation as president, one cannot forget his "Yes we can" rallying cry. In the context of the election, the obvious meaning of "Yes we can" is "Yes, we can win this election." The deeper meaning is "Yes, we can do *anything* we set our minds to do."

President Obama is obviously intelligent (Harvard law graduate), has a richly resonant voice (some have said that he could read the telephone directory, and it would sound good), is skillful at using pauses and voice inflection, and has an imposing stage presence. Yet arguably, his most enduring quality is his ability to energize his "Campaign Warriors" with inspiring battle cries like the simple, three-word "Yes we can." What made President Obama's slogan different than so many political sound bites before it is that it was more than just a catchy tagline; its three words combined to represent things that many voters felt had been lost during the previous eight years: the American can-do feeling, a sense of inclusiveness, and a feeling of self-belief. Many voters didn't feel this way, and they didn't vote for President Obama. But enough of them did to put him in the White House. Like Nike with its "Just do it," *Lord of the Rings*'s Eomer's "To the King" and the French Revolution's "Liberty, equality, fraternity," short, easy-to-understand slogans help us unite in a common cause while at the same time empowering us at the personal level.

✬ ✬ ✬

WARRIOR TACTIC 51 Change your perception of *who you are.*

Another impediment to constructing lofty, uplifting mission statements may be our poor perception of ourselves. To address this problem, let's start by accepting the fact that anatomically, we are all beings with infinite possibilities. Most of the possibilities others have we have too. Science has proven that DNAs vary imperceptibly from one human being to another, regardless of race, place of birth, gender, or age.

Thus, success is not something that is either built in our DNA or is not; rather, it is something we can chase and get. Most importantly, it is something that we can achieve by changing our own perception of who we are. If we perceive we are trustworthy, we become trustworthy. If we perceive we are good in math, we can become good in math. If we perceive we can give good speeches, we can give good speeches. How can that be? It works like this: if you believe you are good at something, that means not only that you can do it, but that you can do it better than many others. Once we raise the bar, we want to be prepared to prove it to others, so we work on improving our performance in that area.

Most of us have the innate ability to do most anything at an above-average level, provided we learn, rehearse, and diligently practice the skill. So by changing our perception to "I *can* do it," we get down to learning, rehearsing, and practicing a skill, eventually becoming above-average performers (even if only barely so), thus fulfilling the promise.

✳ ✳ ✳

WARRIOR TACTIC 52 *Go beyond* **making money and other selfish motives.**

An Ideal Objective type of mission statement must convey a lofty ideal that transcends money-making and selfish motives. It must motivate and inspire employees to the point of accepting their mission with fervor and enthusiasm. Most importantly, the mission statement must have an *altruistic* component. As opposed to selfish self-interest and money-making and the feelings of loyalty and duty, altruism in mission statements should manifest itself as a *selfless concern for the welfare of customers and community*. Don't worry about your employees' acceptance of such altruistic missions, as altruism resonates with most people; it is a traditional virtue in most cultures and a core aspect of all the major religions of the World, including Christianity, Islam, Buddhism, Judaism, Confucianism, Sikhism, and Hinduism.

While I don't suggest elevating Business Warriors' Ideal Objective mission statements to the same level as the lofty ideals of Dr. Martin Luther King Jr. and Mother Teresa, the closer you can get to such lofty ideals, the better. Here are some of the favorite altruistic themes used in my own mission statements:

7. Saving lives.

8. Protecting people from injury.

9. Fostering friendship and understanding among people.

10. Making people more comfortable.

11. Protecting people from financial loss.

12. Helping people make better lives for themselves and their families.

13. Empowering people to be everything that they can be.

✩ ✩ ✩

WARRIOR TACTIC 53 Use fear *positively*.

As we have seen before, fear is a powerful, primitive human emotion as it alerts us to the presence of danger. Over our evolutionary history, we have developed two fear-related traits. The first trait is to detect and overreact to danger. Paradoxically, the second trait is to neglect and dismiss trust and lack of danger. Together, they prime us toward *overestimating the danger posed by people, things, and places and underestimating the trust you can place in people, things, and places.*

People have fears about a whole range of dangers, real and imaginary. How many of us aren't afraid of snakes, spiders, wildfires, pit bulls, and earthquakes? How many of us don't dread going to the dentist, filling in long forms, getting bills for work we never requested, or finding out that something we paid a lot of money for is a fake?

Recessions bring out new fears on top of old ones: the fear of losing your job, fear of being unable to feed your family, fear of losing your business, fear of desperate robbers, and more. Thus, *helping people quell their fears and replacing their fears with hope* should be one of Business Warriors' key approaches to dealing with recessions.

On the opposite side of the coin, find a great weakness in your top competitor's product, which, when fully explained to their customers, will instill fear. Find a way to satisfy the same need as the competitor's product and at the same time reduce or eliminate the cause of fear, and you have a winning combination. As said before, recessions enhance existing fears and bring about new ones. Customers crave reducing fear and want to hope things will get better. Thus, providing that everything else is the same, fear-reducing, hope-inducing products are more likely to succeed during recessions than even during the good times.

EXAMPLE Axxess® Keys

The CreditCard Key Company owned patents for key cards, plastic cards that have flat plastic keys attached in the middle of the cards. These key cards are used as backup keys for homes and cars and can be stored in your wallet just like a credit card. Soon after launch, the company discovered that 20% of their plastic keys were being miscut. They also discovered that even regular metal keys were being miscut. They concluded that the main reason was that the key-cutting machines were difficult to use, thus requiring skilled operators, which most stores didn't have.

The machines were also very noisy, and the grinding process was hurling bits of metal in the air, thus endangering employees and customers alike. That is why key cutting was mostly being done at the back of hardware stores, far away from the customers walking the aisles. Sensing a much bigger opportunity than the plastic key card, the CreditCard Key Company changed its name to Axxess Technologies (a company name and brand I created for them) and set the following as its lofty Ideal Objective statement: *"Be safe with keys that work each and every time."*

Axxess was successful in turning its ideals statement into reality and has since become the largest manufacturer of key blanks and key-cutting machines in the United States.

EXAMPLE FlatPlug® Power Cords

Paige Manufacturing came up with a new type of power cord that had a flat head and a ring to pull it out of the power outlet. The main selling proposition had been that it allowed furniture, TVs, and refrigerators to be pushed snugly against the wall, thus saving floor space. While saving floor space is a good differential advantage, this was not sufficient to make distributors and retailers replace the standard cords from Leviton, the eight-hundred-pound gorilla in the market for power cords. Not wanting to lose this battle, we discovered that many small kids die each year by pulling power cords out of the wall just enough to stick their little fingers in, touch the live prongs, and get electrocuted. The FUD factor we focused on was *the parents' fear that their children will be electrocuted.* The lofty ideal we set for ourselves was *"Save kids' lives."* By trumpeting its safety, the FlatPlug® cord got significant acceptance in the marketplace despite the recession of 1990–1992. FlatPlug® is now one of the leading brands of power cords in the 3-billion-units-per-year marketplace.

✩ ✩ ✩

CHAPTER 14

Mission 4: Develop the New Product

If at first the idea is not absurd, then there is no hope for it.

– Albert Einstein (1879–1955), theoretical physicist

Introduction

Every Ideal Objective must be translated into a killer product. This product is then used to kill the key competitor product's sales by attracting its customers to the new product. In this chapter, we will examine the most effective tactics used to create such killer products.

✦ ✦ ✦

WARRIOR TACTIC 54 Use your products as *weapons*.

The weapons business battles are fought with are the products of the combatants. The winner is the business whose products are purchased by the customers the most. Just as with weapons of war, winning products must be more effective, that is, they must meet more customer wants and needs than their competition, while at the same time must also deliver the best value. For maximum impact and faster market penetration, new products must be surprising, innovative, and have a clearly differentiated look and feel. Just as weapons of war must kill the enemy, so too new products launched during recessions must be capable of killing the key competitors' sales. They must be killer products.

✧ ✧ ✧

WARRIOR TACTIC 55 *Embody your Ideal Objective* **into your products.**

These killer products must support Business Warriors' Ideal Objective. Think of these products as the *physical embodiments of the Ideal Objective.* Successful product design depends on asking the right questions about the proposed product's end users, function, purpose, shape, form, color, texture, assortment, and much more. Thus, product designers must ask many questions such as the following:

- How does the function and purpose of the product help accomplish the Ideal Objective?
- What are the different parts of the product, and how do they work together to help accomplish the Ideal Objective?
- How does the product use shape, form, color, texture, and decoration to help accomplish the Ideal Objective?
- Is the demographic of the customers that would buy this product consistent with the Ideal Objective?
- How well does the product do its job of helping the business reach its Ideal Objective?
- What are the unique features of the product, and are they supportive of the Ideal Objective?

EXAMPLE Rocky Road Ice Cream

Rocky Road ice cream was first created during the Great Depression of 1929 by William Dreyer. He used his wife's sewing shears to cut up chunks of marshmallow and added them and some nuts to chocolate ice cream. Dreyer named his invention Rocky Road in order to deliver something he knew people were craving for even more than ice cream: give folks something to smile about in the midst of the Great Depression. Rocky Road became America's first blockbuster ice cream flavor, and it is still one of the top ten selling flavors. Building on that early success, Dreyer's Grand Ice Cream has become the leading U.S. ice cream producer. The company manufactures premium ice creams and frozen dairy desserts under its Dreyer's and Edy's brands. It also distributes

Haagen-Dazs ice cream and operates the Haagen-Dazs Shoppe Company, which franchises ice cream parlors. Dreyer's sales exceed $1 billion annually, and it is now a subsidiary of Nestle, the largest food company in the world.

✧ ✧ ✧

WARRIOR TACTIC 56 Develop products customers *need*, not merely want.

The product development process used by most companies is based on the deeply flawed assumption that new products must do *what the customers say they want*. Since perception is nine-tenths of reality, what customers say they want becomes the company's reality and that's the product they end up developing. Unfortunately, most customers cannot express what they really *need* because they themselves don't know. One of the reasons for this is that *most people have a built-in belief that there is a limit to the wants that they have the right to fulfill.* They feel that going beyond a certain point in satisfying their wants is a luxury they cannot afford and may not actually deserve. This is especially true during recessions, when most consumers and professional buyers reduce their propensity to purchase.

Thus, when they are asked what they want, *customers usually describe the wants they feel they deserve to have fulfilled.* Another reason for customers' inability to voice what they need is that most people are not able to verbalize their feelings, let alone their deep subconscious needs. Finally, even if they knew what they truly needed, most people are simply not creative enough to be able to describe their needs in detail. Thus, they are incapable of giving product developers enough information to enable them to design the customers' need-fulfilling products.

✧ ✧ ✧

WARRIOR TACTIC 57 Create products that excel in *versatility, affordability, ease of use, and effect.*

When more than one type of weapon is available, soldiers and armies make their weapons selection using four basic value criteria: *versatility, affordability, ease of use,* and *effect.* Similarly, during recessionary times, value becomes of utmost importance, and killer products must distinguish themselves in each one of these areas.

When evaluating the "killing capacity" of a potential new product, the Business Warrior must evaluate every possible use for the product. The reason is simple: the more ways a product can be used, the more versatile it is, and therefore the more value it can deliver to its buyer.

EXAMPLE Elastic Band

Here is an example of a very versatile new product: a five-foot-long elastic band that glows in the dark. You can use it as follows:

1. For fitness exercises

2. To tie down stuff to the roof of a car

3. As a guiding marker in darkness

4. To create wall decorations that glow in the dark

5. As a waistband when jogging outside in the dark

EXAMPLE iPhone vs. RAZR

A very good recent example is iPhone's bypassing Motorola's RAZR during the third quarter of 2008, smack in the middle of a recession. RAZR had been the top-selling mobile phone handset for the previous twelve quarters, despite its 18% failure rate. According to research from the NPD Group, this change in fortunes was due to a "watershed shift in handset design from fashion to fashionable functionality." Simply put, that meant that consumers didn't care that much about looking good anymore – they didn't want to put up with the high failure rate of the RAZR while at the same time preferring the superior functionality of the iPhone.

✦ ✦ ✦

WARRIOR TACTIC 58 Use *green light* sessions to brainstorm for new ideas.

To start the product ideas-generating process, the Business Warrior must brainstorm to create a slew of killer product candidates, always keeping the competing product in their sights. My favorite type of brainstorming is the green light session. It works like this:

- A group of diverse participants representing the target users of the product are brought together.
- The group is presented with the problem.
- Then the participants are asked to
    - Let ideas flow
    - Be as creative as they can be
    - Be accepting of all ideas even if they're way-out
    - Build on the good ideas of others
    - Refrain from criticizing other participants' ideas

This process creates an atmosphere of cooperation and teamsmanship and opens up everyone's creativity gates without the fear of being criticized or looking silly.

A major problem encountered when selecting participants for green light sessions is that the vast majority of the people employed by businesses are chosen based on their willingness to follow orders, not on their ability to think out-of-the-box. They are neither creative enough nor adventurous enough to dream up breakthrough ideas. Thus by necessity Business Warriors must seek participants that are maverick thinkers from *outside* of their own businesses.

After each green light session is completed, Business Warriors must sort through the potential killer products generated using the four basic criteria mentioned earlier: *versatility, cost efficiency, ease of use,* and, most importantly, their *potential to kill the sales of the target competitor's product.* Any potential product that does not take advantage of a major flaw in the key competing product, and thus has no chance of killing it, must be removed from future consideration.

✼ ✼ ✼

WARRIOR TACTIC 59 Determine what the customers truly need *before they themselves find out.*

Another problem is that when developing new products, Business Warriors must determine what customers really need *before the customers become consciously aware of their needs.* Business Warriors must race ahead of their customers' conscious realization because once they realize what they need, that need instantly becomes a want, and thus they are likely to act upon it. They might tell your competitors about it, thus giving them a leg up on developing the need-satisfying product before the Business Warriors do. Worse, if the customers conceived of the need-fulfilling product first, then Business Warriors will not be able to obtain patent protection for the invention because in the United States, patents are granted to the first person to conceive an invention, not to the first one to file the patent application for it. You will read more about this importance of patent protection and other forms of intellectual property protection in later chapters. The bottom line is that Business Warriors must develop new products and product features that fulfill needs *before* the customers themselves are aware they have the needs.

✼ ✼ ✼

WARRIOR TACTIC 60 Launch new businesses with *only one* killer product.

Similar to these surprising new weapons of war discussed earlier in this book, *virtually all great businesses have been launched based on just one killer product.* That's right: *just one killer product!* That's how Amazon, Apple, Avon, Bank of America, Barnes & Noble, Best Buy, Campbell Soup, Caterpillar, Chevron, Coca-Cola, Dell, DuPont, Eastman Kodak, Edison, Estee Lauder, FedEx, Foot Locker, Ford, Gap, Gateway, General Electric, General Motors, Goodyear, H. J. Heinz, Home Depot, Intel, IBM, Johnson & Johnson, Kellogg's, Levi Strauss, Marriott, Mattel, McDonalds, Microsoft, Motorola, Nike, Nordstrom, Office Depot, PepsiCo, Procter & Gamble, RadioShack, Reebok, Sears, Staples, Starbucks, Wal-Mart, and practically every single other Fortune 500 company got its start.

Why just *one* killer product and not two, three, or even more? Here are the reasons:

A. The complexity of designing, financing, manufacturing, and marketing new products increases exponentially with the number of new products involved.

B. Most companies, especially start-ups, have a limited number of employees and machines and a limited amount of money and materials that can be devoted to new product developments, thus not delivering immediate cash. Under such circumstances, it is hard enough to get resources allocated to one product; it is infinitely harder to get resources for many products at the same time.

C. During recessions, just as in war, investors, suppliers, customers, bankers, and employees are less able and less willing to listen to new product pitches and make complex decisions involving higher risks.

When it comes to new product development, the old KISS principle ("Keep It Simple, Stupid") applies: one killer product, one killer story. Period.

EXAMPLE Axxess® Keys

In line with its lofty Ideal Objective *"Be safe with keys that work each and every time,"* Axxess developed as its weapon a revolutionary new product: a foolproof key-cutting machine that was easy to operate, quiet, and safe for the operator and the customers. The company succeeded in developing a key-cutting robot that cuts both plastic and metal keys perfectly, each and every time. It is so easy to use that regular employees in supermarkets and mass merchandisers can operate it. Women, who buy over 70% of all the keys, no longer have to go into the back-of-the-store dark corners at the back of hardware stores to have keys made. They can now have them cut where they usually shop: at the service counters of brightly lit supermarkets and mass merchandisers. The robot cutters use proprietary key blank cartridges available only from Axxess. This tried-and-true razor-and-blades business model has stood the company well. Axxess has become the largest supplier of key blanks in the country.

✧ ✧ ✧

WARRIOR TACTIC 61 Price products based on the *value delivered to customers, rather than* the cost to make them.

In times of recession, setting the right price for the products is of the most critical tasks facing the Business Warrior. Start by identifying those products that can deliver demonstrable value to customers, then price them not based on your cost but on the *value delivered to the customers.* If selected properly, most products developed and promoted according to the principles explained in the previous chapters should merit *value-based pricing.*

The prices companies charge for their products and services are often *too low.* This is because in the vast majority of cases, companies set the price they ask customers to pay for their products based on their own *cost for the products.* Unfortunately, most of us have been brought up to believe that one of the most important things in life is to be fair to others. I call it "the fairness doctrine." Our parents say it, our teachers teach it, our churches preach it, and our governments extol it. Using this fairness doctrine, the typical pricing rationale goes something like this: "It costs me $10 at wholesale to purchase this item. I am happy to make a $2 profit, so I will sell it for $12." Thus, if the customer would have been willing to pay $15, we missed out on making the extra $3 profit.

Although price is an important consumer motivator during recessions, *it is not the main motivator.* In fact, it has been shown that during recessions, consumers are more interested in *the value received* rather than in the price paid. There are several problems with the fairness doctrine when it comes to product pricing. First, there is no such thing as a *universal right price* for anything.

Value-based pricing sets selling prices on the perceived value to the customer, rather than on the actual cost of the product, the market price, competitors' prices, or the historical price for the product. Value-based prices reflect the specific value delivered, measured using metrics such as number of users, number of annual transactions, size of revenues, and cost savings.

If you do not make the case as to the benefits of your product versus the competition so that you can justify value-based pricing and your customer cannot make it either, who do you think will make the case? Your competitors, of course. They will take advantage of the knowledge vacuum and fill it with their own product benefits, naturally biased in their favor rather than yours.

Let's examine the concept of measuring product benefits, otherwise referred to as product metrics. There are three types of product metrics:

- **Short-term measures**
  These include weekly sales reports, monthly attrition reports, customer feedback forms, etc.
- **Long-term measures**
  These include departmental goals achieved, executive behavior change, changes in public image, etc.
- **Client-specific measures**
  Measures unique to a company's particular culture and business such as additional business sold by a call center, reduction in repetitive repair calls by an appliance company, renewed policies by an insurance firm, etc.

Business Warriors must use product metrics to prove to their customers that theirs is a "need to have" product, that they can reduce the number of service calls, reduce the number of returns, etc.

EXAMPLE Coffee Shop

Let's say I own a coffee shop on the south side of a street and my competitor owns a coffee shop on the north side of the same street. For various reasons, my sidewalk gets a lot of foot traffic, but his doesn't. Our rents are the same, our coffee beans cost us the same, our staffs get paid the same. Should we price our coffee the same? Using the fairness doctrine, we should. But is this smart? Of course not. My foot traffic is such that even if my price for a cup of coffee is double that of my competitor's, most of my customers would still buy it because of the convenience of not having to cross the street. Besides, most of my customers don't even know what my competitor's price is. Thus, rather than pricing my cup of coffee based on my cost, I can price it based on the *value my customers receive from the cup of coffee conveniently purchased on their way, without having to cross the street.* The act of crossing the street and walking to the competitor's coffee shop has certain costs associated with it. It takes extra time to get there, it exposes the customers to the danger of crossing a busy street, and once there they may find a long line.

EXAMPLE Axxess® Keys

The price recommended by Axxess® for a key perfectly cut using the Axxess® 2000 robot is over $1, *over twice the going price for imperfectly cut (20% of the time) keys in hardware stores.* A small premium considering the inconvenience of going back to recut the key or, worse, finding yourself stuck in an empty parking lot late at night locked out of your car with a spare key that doesn't work.

EXAMPLE FlatPlug® Power Cords

These power cords sell for more than twice the price of standard cords. Keeping our children safe is more important than saving a few dollars, isn't it? The cost of manufacturing FlatPlug cords is virtually the same as standard ones. The profits are high and the cause is worthy, a perfect combination.

✫ ✫ ✫

CHAPTER 15

Mission 5: Protect the New Product

Before then any man might instantly use what another had invented; so that the inventor had no special advantage from his own invention. The patent system changed this; secured to the inventor, for a limited time, the exclusive use of his invention; and thereby added the fuel of interest to the fire of genius, in the discovery and production of new and useful things.

– Abraham Lincoln (1809–1865), sixteenth president of the United States, in his second lecture on Discoveries and Inventions, Jacksonville, Illinois, February 11, 1859

Introduction

Now that we have built the new product, we need to protect it from being copied and imitated. Once launched, a killer product will not be ignored by the competitor, whose product sales are targeted by it for destruction. The competitor, like enemies in war, will mount a strong defense. If it is the product leader in the marketplace, the competitor will also likely mount a strong counterattack. One important way to protect against such counterattacks is for the Business Warrior to have demonstrable product superiority and to continuously communicate it to the target audience, the customers. Unfortunately, this is not enough because most competitors faced with clearly superior competing products eventually copy those products' key features and add them to their own products. Such mimicking leads to a loss of differential advantage for the now-not-so-killer product. Eventually the hunter, the killer product, becomes the hunted.

It has been estimated that 80% of all new products fail within the first six months from launch, even though most of them pass through conventional market testing such as focus groups on their way to market. A big contributor to these failures is new products' chronic inability to defend themselves against competitive counterattacks. The statistics are grim as billions of dollars are wasted each year in failed new product launching efforts.

Instead of thinking several moves in advance, like chess players and military leaders do, most businesses do not think far enough ahead about what their competitors' next moves will be. Without protection and without preparation against the almost-inevitable counterattacks from riled competitors, many businesspeople lose new product battles soon after they are launched.

☆ ☆ ☆

WARRIOR TACTIC 62 Obtain *patents* on novel and unique products.

Patents are by far the most important defensive weapons available to Business Warriors. Patents have a special place in the history of the United States, and the connection between patents and the Founding Fathers goes deep. Very early on, the Founding Fathers realized that "Yankee ingenuity" was a unique resource of the American people, and it had to be protected. When the United States **Patent and Trademark Office** celebrated its one hundredth birthday, a bust was dedicated to Thomas Jefferson (1743–1826), third president of the United States, who had been its first patent examiner and an inventor before becoming president.

A patent is the grant of a property right to the inventor of a novel and unique product or process. Patents can only be issued by the U.S. Patent and Trademark Office operated by the U.S. federal government. Generally, the term of a new patent is twenty years from the date on which the application for the patent was filed in the United States or, in special cases, from the date an earlier related application was filed. U.S. patent grants are effective only within the United States, U.S. territories, and U.S. possessions.

The right conferred by the patent grant is "the right to exclude others from making, using, offering for sale or selling" the invention in the United States or "importing" the invention into the United States. Contrary to popular belief, what is granted is not the right to make, use, offer for sale, sell, or import patented products; rather, it is the right to *exclude* others from making, using, offering for sale, selling, or importing products using the invention. Once a patent is issued, the patentee must enforce the patent without aid of the U.S. Patent and Trademark Office.

There are three types of patents:

1. *Utility patents* may be granted to anyone who invents or discovers any new and useful process, machine, article of manufacture or composition of matter, or any new and useful improvement thereof.

2. *Design patents* may be granted to anyone who invents a new, original, and ornamental design for an article of manufacture.

3. *Plant patents* may be granted to anyone who invents or discovers and asexually reproduces any distinct and new variety of plant.

It typically costs $10,000 or less to obtain a U.S. patent, and it takes two to four years, depending on how busy the U.S. Patent Office is and the subject matter covered by the patent. However, for less than $200, an inventor can file a provisional patent application and be protected for one year. During that year, the inventor can determine the feasibility of making and marketing products based on the invention. Before the year is up, the inventor must either file a permanent application and spend up to $10,000 as indicated before or abandon the invention to the public domain.

Unfortunately, for reasons that are too many to mention, a majority of businesspeople do not understand these wonderful government-issued defensive weapons and don't use them. They believe that patents are ineffective as weapons and are too expensive to obtain, so they ignore them altogether.

Let's address the issue of cost first. As mentioned before, the typical patent can be obtained for under $10,000. This is a drop in the bucket when compared with the very high cost of battling the competition by lowering prices or carrying out expensive advertising campaigns.

Over the years, I have been fortunate to obtain patents for several products of my own and for tens of products for client companies. I have also been successfully involved in several patent infringement lawsuits. Based on this firsthand experience, I firmly believe that there are no defensive weapons more powerful than patents. No Business Warrior should ever go into battle with new products or new product features without first protecting them with patents. Period.

✵ ✵ ✵

WARRIOR TACTIC 63 Enforce your patents through *litigation.*

Patents are only as good as the Business Warriors' willingness and ability to enforce them. Unfortunately, unlike other forms of intellectual property, patents can only be enforced through civil lawsuits. There are no criminal penalties for patent infringement in the United States, thus Business Warriors cannot get Uncle Sam to help them find against infringers.

For a U.S. patent, infringement lawsuits must be brought to a United States federal court. In such actions patent owners seek monetary compensation for past infringement and an injunction to stop the infringers.

Typically, patents have several claims. In order to prove infringement, the patent owner must establish that the accused infringer practices all of the requirements of at least one of these claims. It is important to note that the patent rights may not be limited to what is stated in the claims; their scope may be enlarged by the doctrine of equivalents. This means that an infringer cannot get around a patent by making simple changes to the product.

✵ ✵ ✵

WARRIOR TACTIC 64 Obtain patent and trademark *infringement litigation insurance.*

To protect against the possibility of having to pay for attorneys to defend claims of patent or trademark infringement, it is best to obtain infringement insurance. Such insurance is also available for covering the legal expenses of lawsuits brought by patent and trademark owners against infringers. Infringement litigation insurance must be purchased before the insured knows that someone is about to sue or, if he is a patent or trademark owner, before he finds out that someone is infringing his patent or trademark.

WARRIOR TACTIC 65 Try to settle patent litigation out of court.

Over 90% of the patent infringement cases get settled without ever going to trial. Here's why: although for cases that get to trial about two-thirds of the time the patent owner wins, the battles are typically long and arduous. They sap significant time from the Business Warriors, which is time that may be better used in battling in the marketplace rather than in the courts.

WARRIOR TACTIC 66 Hire infringement litigation attorneys on *contingency.*

Business Warriors that own or are exclusive licensees of strong patents or trademarks can pretty readily find law firms that will work on a contingency basis, that is, they don't have to pay a nickel toward the cost of litigation until they receive judgment money. Patent and trademark infringers, on the other hand, must pay full fees and costs to the attorneys defending them.

It currently costs an average of $3 million to defend a patent infringement lawsuit, enough to put a company out of business, and many infringers end up doing just that. Make no mistake: patents are the most important competitive weapons in a Business Warrior's arsenal.

WARRIOR TACTIC 67 Register trademarks for *all* important brand names.

A trademark is a word, name, symbol, or device that is used in trade with goods to indicate the source of the goods and to distinguish them from the goods of others. A service mark is the same as a trademark except that it identifies and distinguishes the source of a service rather than a product. The terms "trademark" and "mark" are commonly used to refer to both trademarks and service marks.

Trademark rights may be used to prevent others from using a confusingly similar mark, but not to prevent others from making the same goods or from selling the same goods or services under a clearly different mark. Trademarks that are used in interstate or foreign commerce may be registered with the United States Patent and Trademark Office.

✮ ✮ ✮

WARRIOR TACTIC 68 Create *strong* brand names.

Strong, defensible brand names have several characteristics:

FACT 1 Good brand names are *short*.

Branding experts believe that a good brand name should have no more than seven letters.

EXAMPLES

- Acura

- Adidas

- Armani

- Equal

- Guess

- Ivory

- Nike

- Splenda

- Toyota

FACT 2 Good brand names start with *strong, explosive sounds.*

EXAMPLES

- Coca-Cola

- Kodak

- Pepsi

- Starbucks

- Target

- Zantac

FACT 3 Good brand names conjure the *benefits* from using the product.

EXAMPLES

- Kool-Aid – Soft drink products

- Mr. Clean – Household cleaner

- Nutri-Grain – Health bars

- Staples – Retail stores selling office products

- Sunkist – Oranges

EXAMPLE NutraSweet® and Equal®

At one time, my brother and I owned Bionex, an early pioneer in the engineered foods industry. One of our more interesting projects was to help launch the new sweetener aspartame into the marketplace. The product's owner, Searle, realized that the product's technical name "aspartame" didn't give the consumer any idea as to what it was. Eventually, it came up with two consumer-friendly brand names for aspartame: *NutraSweet®*, when used as a sweetening ingredient in foods and beverages, and *Equal®*, when used as a tabletop sweetener. These two brand names carry obvious, simple-to-understand meanings: *NutraSweet* denotes "nutritious and sweet," and *Equal* denotes "same as sugar." Both Equal and NutraSweet became huge successes for Searle, with sales exceeding $2 billion annually.

EXAMPLES Other successful brand names

Here are some of very successful brand names I have created for clients and for my own companies by using the tactics described above:

- Axxess® – Robotic key-cutting machines and key blanks

- FlatPlug® – A flathead power cord

- InstaPlay® – A system to launch video games instantly

- Memorabilia Card™ – A trading card with a piece of memorabilia attached

- MotorVac® – A vacuum cleaner for car engines

- Players To Watch® – A system to track top athletes

- SuperElite® – A testing and training system for super-elite athletes

- UltraSafe® – An ultra-safe syringe

- XCaper® – A fire-escape smoke mask

✿ ✿ ✿

WARRIOR TACTIC 69 Register *copyrights.*

Copyrights give the creator of an original work of authorship exclusive rights to control its distribution for a certain time period, after which the work enters the public domain. In my opinion, unless you are a writer, composer, or software developer, copyrights are a poor way to try to protect new products.

☆ ☆ ☆

WARRIOR TACTIC 70 Protect *trade secrets.*

A trade secret is a formula, practice, process, design, instrument, pattern, or compilation of information that is not generally known or reasonably ascertainable. Trade secrets are also referred to as confidential information and classified information. My experience with trade secrets has been mixed. On occasion, I have discovered that internal processes and concepts that were confidential to my companies somehow found their way into competitors' hands. My experience has been that absent a nondisclosure agreement signed by both parties and/or without being able to name a specific individual that disclosed the secret information, it is virtually impossible to do anything about such disclosures.

On the other hand, when the reverse is the case and there is proof that trade secrets have been stolen, the repercussions on the perpetrators can be very serious. Trade secret theft is prosecuted under the Economic Espionage Act of 1996, and it carries serious criminal penalties involving long prison sentences and huge monetary fines. Section 1832 of this act punishes the theft, misappropriation, wrongful conversion, duplication, alteration, destruction, etc., of a trade secret. The section also punishes attempts and conspiracies.

☆ ☆ ☆

WARRIOR TACTIC 71 Prepare for potential lawsuits *before* they happen.

During past recessions, the amount of litigation between businesses increased significantly. While it is rare that litigation is the answer to business disputes, as most of them can be settled through negotiation, litigation is a fact of life in the United States, especially during recessions. Threats of litigation must not be ignored. It is important to act quickly and decisively whenever the possibility of litigation arises. Any threat of litigation must be reported to Business Warriors' CEOs immediately. Business Warriors should select litigation attorneys well in advance of potential litigation and have them become knowledgeable about the business. The attorneys should develop written policies on how to deal with potential litigation and how to best protect Business Warriors' trade secrets.

CHAPTER 16

Mission 6: Execute the Battle Plan

Vision without execution is hallucination.

– Thomas Edison (1847–1931), American inventor and businessman

Introduction

In this chapter, we learn the key tactics needed in order to successfully execute the six missions of the SWIPPE™ recession battle plan quickly and efficiently.

✵ ✵ ✵

WARRIOR TACTIC 72 Develop a *detailed* battle plan.

As in war, it is extremely important to kick off the campaign to kill the key competitor's product by first developing a detailed battle plan. Once started, most competitive wars become progressively less manageable, less controllable, and less susceptible to direction. This is especially true of business actions taken under the duress experienced during recessions. This is a time when business participants – be they customers, suppliers, employees, and even advisors – are more stressed out, more emotional, and less objective. They are confused, and possibly even scared by the continuous stream of bad news in the press, negative reports from the salesmen out in the field, and disquieting rumors heard at industry events. A detailed plan in which everyone is accountable is an absolute must if you want to keep the six SWIPPE™ missions on track despite these challenges.

The following is the recommended sequence of steps to create a SWIPPE™ battle plan:

STEP 1

Break down the battle plan into tasks. Each task must take no less than ten elapsed days and no longer than thirty elapsed days.

STEP 2

Break down each task into subtasks. Each subtask must take no less than one elapsed day and no more than three elapsed days.

STEP 3

At the very least, the plan must show for each task the following information:

- Task number

- Task description

- Task team leader

- Task team members

- For each subtask

    o Subtask team leader

    o Subtask team members

    o Man-hours of work for each subtask team member

    o Subtask start date

    o Subtask completion date

    o Subtask resources needed: men, machines, materials, methods, money

✫ ✫ ✫

WARRIOR TACTIC 73 Base all actions on *reliable* intelligence.

If surprise is the disease, intelligence is the cure. It is virtually impossible to devise a plan of attack against a competitor without knowing its strengths and weaknesses. We have discussed earlier in this book the importance of determining a competitor's weaknesses. Now let's look at an example of what constitutes good intelligence and how to gather and use it effectively.

✫ ✫ ✫

WARRIOR TACTIC 74 Use *surprise and deception.*

We know from military war strategy that if the defender has enough time and space in which to recover, the aggressor inevitably reaches a point at which he must himself go on the defense. Thus, time is almost always on the side of the *defender.*

We also know from war strategy that in order to give defenders the least amount of time and space, we must use *surprise and deception.* When we are able to attack, we must seem unable to do so; when using our troops, we must appear inactive; when we are near, we must make the enemy believe we are far away; and when far away, we must make them believe we are near.

The backbone of surprise is *fusing speed with secrecy.* Surprise very frequently has ended a war with a single stroke, thus may well be the most essential component of victory. As with most other key strategic tactics of military war, these tactics also apply to business battles.

WARRIOR TACTIC 75 Hold *weekly* status meetings.

Probably the most important tool for keeping a battle plan on track is having regular status review meetings not less than once a week, attended by all the key team members. Meetings should always start with a reading of the Ideal Objective for the current battle. The participants must be reminded again who the key competitor of the company is for each one of its products and what initiatives are being undertaken in order to attack those competitors' products' sales. Only after this preamble should the meeting continue with the rest of the agenda. Business Warriors must always keep their followers motivated by the drive to destroy the key competitor's sales. Everything else follows.

✵ ✵ ✵

WARRIOR TACTIC 76 Recession-proof your *Web sites.*

During recessions, customers are less patient with difficult-to-understand instructions and long-winded explanations. In the face of economic uncertainty and hardships, customers seek simple, straight-to-the-point answers, and most of all, truthfulness. This is most important when it comes to a business's brochures, ads, and Web sites. Of these, the area most lacking in my experience is the Web sites. Here are a few words of wisdom that have held me in good stead on several Web site development projects:

- Improve site navigation.

- Streamline the buying process.

- Improve the Web site's load time.

- Improve the search engine optimization (SEO).

- Improve the search engine marketing (SEM).

- Simplify the content.

- Reduce visual clutter.

- Optimize landing pages.

- Improve site usability.

- Add site features and functionality that are appropriate and relevant to your site and business and that enhance the user experience.

- Use social media to engage, interact, and build relationships with new and existing customers and to reach them *where they are* versus relying on them coming to you.

- Use Webinars as a tool to save travel costs and time.

✧ ✧ ✧

WARRIOR TACTIC 77 Be very careful when dealing with companies in *recession-prone industries.*

There are some industries that are particularly hard hit during recessions. Here is a list of these industries, based on their performance during past recessions:

- Auto

- Banking

- Construction

- Consumer appliances

- Finance

- Furniture

- Luxury consumer goods

- Machinery

- Steel

- Telecommunications

- Textiles
- Travel

Be careful when dealing with companies in these industries, *both as suppliers and as customers,* as many companies in these industries go bankrupt during recessions. If that happens and they are your customers, even in the best-case scenario, you are unlikely to ever collect all the money due to you if you sold them goods on credit. If they go bankrupt and they are your suppliers, you may lose your advance deposits, critical shipments, and credibility with your own customers.

✡ ✡ ✡

WARRIOR TACTIC 78 Launch the new product with *lots of noise.*

Once the product is developed and properly protected with patents, trademarks, copyrights, and trade secrets, Business Warriors must spring the news on their customers with a great deal of surprise and with great fanfare. When customers and prospects first learn about the new product or feature, they must feel as if it was their birthday, the Fourth of July, and Christmas all rolled into one!

EXAMPLE Launch of the Mac by Apple

An excellent example of a memorable new product launch was the 1984 introduction of the original Macintosh computer by Apple. Steve Jobs, the founder and CEO of Apple, wanted to launch the Macintosh with an inspiring commercial that was as revolutionary as the product itself. He loved the Orwellian tagline "Why 1984 won't be like 1984" created by his ad agency Chiat-Day (now part of *TBWA\Chiat\Day*) and hired the now-famous Ridley Scott to direct the commercial.

Ridley Scott was based in London at the time. He needed a cast of two hundred oppressed, downtrodden, baldheaded workers, so he recruited dozens of authentic British skinheads for $125 dollars a day each. For the part of the young heroine who had to spin with a very heavy sledgehammer, he cast an accomplished discus thrower.

The commercial was aired during the Super Bowl at the first commercial break after the second half kickoff, and it was a resounding success. Most evening news shows over the following few days featured the ad, thus giving Apple over five million dollars of free publicity. The commercial won many awards including the best commercial of the decade. The Macintosh itself quickly became a cultural icon and continues to be a leading computer brand with a special cache to this day. I was one of the first buyers of the original Macintosh and loved it so much that I gave several away as gifts to my closest friends and associates.

This is the kind of emotional impact Business Warriors must strive for. This type of gutsy thinking and execution is what differentiates amazing product launches from the run-of-the-mill introductions we are all too familiar with: tepid press releases, followed by timid ads that say very little, mean even less, and move no one.

✿ ✿ ✿

WARRIOR TACTIC 79 Use other recession-battling tactics if applicable to your business.

In addition to using the SWIPPE™ system's warlike tactics, there are other more standard tactics Business Warriors must consider undertaking during recessions. These are "equalizers" that will ensure no openings are available for the competition to criticize and attack the Business Warrior's business:

- Act like a helpful consultant.

- Be a tougher negotiator.

- Boost advertising.

- Create strategic partnerships to cut costs.

- Create strategic partnerships to generate new sales leads.

- Cut capital-intensive projects.

- Downgrade the acceptable customer profile.

- Drop the shipping fees.

- Extend the products' usability by offering repair services and warranties.

- Extend customer support hours.

- Focus on family values.

- Focus on fewer target markets.

- Foster continuous and repeat business from current customers.

- Give customers more than their money's worth.

- Give customers free advice.

- Give customers rebates.

- Instill confidence in the business and its products.

- Make acquisitions.

- Offer temporary price promotions.

- Outsource internal operations to competent subject matter experts.

- Provide leadership.

- Provide outsourced services to larger players in the same industry.

- Push multipurpose products over specialized products.

- Quell customer fears about spending money.

- Reactivate dormant accounts.

- Reactivate old leads.

- Reactivate past customers.

- Reduce thresholds for quantity discounts.

- Save customers money.

- Sell complementary products.

- Sell supplementary products.

- Set up a referral reward program for existing customers.

- Stop being a prima donna.

- Use public relations (PR) communications rather than paid ads.

✷ ✷ ✷

WARRIOR TACTIC 80 Carry out *rehearsals and simulations.*

Just as the military carries out exercises before battles, so too Business Warriors need to rehearse their battle plans before launching into action. The best method for doing this is through computer simulations. Everyone is familiar with the first computer simulation of broad mass appeal: the spreadsheet. With a few keystrokes, users can revise a spreadsheet containing a financial forecast in seconds. Unfortunately, to carry out more complex, multidimensional scenarios requires multiple interconnected spreadsheets and quite a bit of skill with advanced features of the spreadsheet programs. It is tedious and time-consuming work, prone to errors that are very difficult to detect. There have been numerous publicized cases where major forecasts were erroneous due to such small undetected errors.

A number of vendors have created complex simulations that enable users to feed their data through human-friendly interfaces without requiring them to have advance knowledge in using spreadsheets. In late 2009, Business Warrior Institute is planning to launch on www.businesswarriorinstitute.com an easy-to-use battle simulator specifically designed to simulate SWIPPE™ battle plans.

✷ ✷ ✷

APPENDIX 1

Companies included in the Dow Jones Industrial Average (2008)

Company	Year Founded	During Recessionary Period	Industry
3M	1902	Yes	Diversified industrials
Alcoa	1886	Yes	Aluminum
American Express	1850		Consumer finance
AT&T	1983	Yes	Telecommunication
Bank of America	1929	Yes	Institutional and retail banking
Boeing	1916	Yes	Aerospace and defense
Caterpillar	1890	Yes	Construction and mining equipment
Chevron Corporation	1879	Yes	Oil and gas
Citigroup	1812		Banking
Coca-Cola	1886	Yes	Beverages
DuPont	1802		Commodity chemicals
ExxonMobil	1870	Yes	Integrated oil and gas
General Electric	1892	Yes	Conglomerate
General Motors	1908	Yes	Automobiles
Hewlett-Packard	1935	Yes	Diversified computer systems
Home Depot	1978	Yes	Home improvement retailers
Intel	1968		Semiconductors
IBM	1896	Yes	Computer services
Johnson & Johnson	1886	Yes	Pharmaceuticals
JPMorgan Chase	1871	Yes	Banking
Kraft Foods	1909	Yes	Food processing
McDonald's	1955	Yes	Restaurants and bars
Merck	1891	Yes	Pharmaceuticals
Microsoft	1975	Yes	Software
Pfizer	1849		Pharmaceuticals
Procter & Gamble	1837	Yes	Non-Durable household products
United Technologies Corporation	1929	Yes	Aerospace, HVAC, elevators
Verizon Communications	1983	Yes	Telecommunication
Wal-Mart	1962	Yes	Retailers
Walt Disney	1929	Yes	Broadcasting and entertainment

APPENDIX 2
Recession-Proof Industries

According to *Forbes* magazine's recently released issue "The Other Economy," here are the industries that are most likely to survive recessions unscathed:

- Air-conditioning/heating
- Airliner maintenance
- Auctions
- Biosciences
- Career / job search / life coaching
- Cosmetics
- Debt collection
- Discount retailers
- Education
- Emergency services
- Energy
- Entertainment
- Farming
- Federal government
- Food chains
- Funeral homes

- Health care services

- Home repair and maintenance

- Insurance

- Liquor

- Medical services / health care

- Occupational therapy

- Pet and pet supplies stores

- Pharmaceuticals

- Pharmacies

- Physical therapy

- Plastics

- Security / alarm services

- Software / technology solutions

- Soup and convenience food

- Tax preparation / simplification

- Tobacco

- Vehicle repair and maintenance

APPENDIX 3

U.S. Recessions

A Short History of Recent Recessions

Recession of 1973–1975

This recession, as many others before and after, at first manifested itself through catastrophically decreasing investment purchases. This was also the immediate cause of the Great Depression of the 1930's. There were prior causes, such as the high interest rates due to restrictive monetary policy, but it was the drop in investment purchases that caused most of the damage to the economy. This decrease in investment purchases was seen in most components of investment: manufacturing equipment, industrial buildings, residential housing, and business inventories. The unemployment rate jumped from 5% to nearly 9% in about a year and a half. Congress enacted a tax cut program. This included a one-time rebate to taxpayers of 10% of their 1974 personal income tax, up to a maximum of $200. There was also a permanent tax reduction that affected the tax withholding through the rest of the year. There was also an increase in the business investment tax credits. To accompany the economic stimulus of the tax cuts, there was an increase in state and local governments' funding that was used to create public service jobs. The federal budget deficit jumped from $25 billion to $102 billion. Enticed by the prospect of an economy that would be once again growing, investment purchases increased, and the economy recovered.

Recession of 1980–1982

The cause of this recession was most likely the tight money policy that the fed carried out to kill the chronic inflation that had developed in the U.S. economy during the 1970s. The result was a drastic reduction in investment, which in turn caused rising unemployment. In order to stimulate the economy, President Reagan pushed through a major tax cut, together with cuts in some federal government purchases, but significant increases in defense spending. These measures increased the federal government's deficits, yet the expectations of economic recovery and growth induced a higher level of investment purchases, and eventually, the economy recovered.

Recession of 1990–1992

On Black Monday of October 1987, the Dow Jones Industrial Average dropped by an unprecedented 22.6%. This collapse was larger than that of 1929, yet it was handled well by the economy, and the stock market started recovering. However, the savings and loans industry started collapsing in 1989, putting the savings of millions of Americans at risk. The panic withdrawal of deposits that followed led to a sharp recession. By 1990, the economic malaise deepened with the beginning of the Gulf War, the resulting 1990 jump in the price of oil, which in turn increased inflation and President Bush's modest tax increases. Eventually, the Gulf War ended; markets stabilized; the election of President Clinton brought renewed hope to the consuming public, which increased its spending; and the economy recovered.

Recession of 2000–2002

This recession began in March 2000 when the National Association of Securities Dealers Automated Quotations (NASDAQ) crashed following the collapse of the dot-com bubble. The Dow Jones Industrial Average (DJIA) was relatively unscathed by the NASDAQ's crash until the September 11, 2001, terrorist attacks, after which the DJIA suffered its worst one-day point loss and biggest one-week losses in history up to that point. Corporate profits peaked in the mid-2000 and then started declining. As a result, the private investment in plant and equipment, new house construction, and inventory started declining. The discount rate fell substantially, and the T-bill rate fell with it. Unemployment began to rise. Due to large layoffs and increased outsourcing, many formerly high-paid manufacturing and professional employees were forced into much-lower-paid jobs. The market rebounded, only to crash once more in the final two quarters of 2002. In the final three quarters of 2003, the market finally rebounded and stabilized, investment purchases started growing again, and the recession ended.

Recession of 2008–

Like all recessions before it, the basic business dynamics have not changed during the recession that started in 2008. We are witnessing the same signs, the same pains, and the same challenges: higher unemployment, lower demand, tighter credit, and increased competition.

BIBLIOGRAPHY

Bate, Nicholas. *Beat the 2008 Recession: A Blueprint for Business Survival.* Infinite Ideas Limited, 2008.

Benson, Herbert and Miriam Z. Klipper. *The Relaxation Response.* Expanded Updated Edition. Harper Paperbacks, 2000.

Bruner, Robert F. and Sean D. Carr. *The Panic of 1907: Lessons Learned from the Market's Perfect Storm.* John Wiley & Sons, 2007.

Collins, James C. and Jerry I. Porras. *Built to Last: Successful Habits of Visionary Companies.* Harper Business, 1997.

Colvin, Geoff. *Talent Is Overrated: What Really Separates World-Class Performers from Everybody Else.* Portfolio Hardcover, 2008.

Cunningham, Brian T. *Never Give Up!: Life Lessons of a Successful Entrepreneur.* iUniverse Inc., 2008.

DeVos, Rich. *Ten Powerful Phrases for Positive People.* Center Street, 2008.

Feynman, Richard P. *What Do You Care What Other People Think?: Further Adventures of a Curious Character.* W. W. Norton, 1988.

Gladwell, Malcolm. *Outliers: The Story of Success.* Little, Brown and Company, 2008.

Hall, Gordon. *The Crash of 1987.* Johnson County Publishers, 1987.

Hart, Rupert. *Recession Storming: Thriving in Downturns through Superior Marketing, Pricing, and Product Strategies,* Amazon.com, 2008.

Kindleberger, Charles P. and Robert Z. Aliber. *Manias, Panics and Crashes: A History of Financial Crises.* John Wiley & Sons Inc., 2005.

Kourdi, Jeremy. *Surviving a Downturn*. A & C Black, London, 2007.

Marcinko, Richard. *Leadership Secrets of the Rogue Warrior*. Pocket Handbooks, 1996.

Marcinko, Richard. *The Rogue Warrior's Strategy for Success*. Pocket Handbooks, 1997.

Navarro, Peter. *The Well-Timed Strategy: Managing the Business Cycle for Competitive Advantage*. Wharton School Publishing, 2006.

Pollan, Stephen M. and Mark Levine. *Your Recession Handbook*. William Morrow & Company, 1991.

Ries, Al and Jack Trout. *Marketing Warfare*. McGraw-Hill, 1985.

− − −. *Positioning: The Battle for Your Mind*. McGraw-Hill, 2001.

− − −. *The 22 Immutable Laws of Marketing: Violate Them at Your Own Risk!* HarperCollins, 1994.

Samli, A. Coskun. *Counterturbulence Marketing*. Quorum Handbooks, 1993.

Sigafoos, Robert A. *Absolutely Positively Overnight!: The Story of Federal Express*. Mass Market Paperback, 1984.

Trout, Jack. *Trout on Strategy: Capturing Mindshare, Conquering Markets*. McGraw-Hill, 2004.

Tuller, Lawrence W. *Recession-Proof Your Business*, Bob Adams Inc., 1991.

Van Hecke, Madeleine L. *Blind Spots: Why Smart People Do Dumb Things*. Prometheus Books, 2007.

Williams, Pete. *Card Sharks: How Upper Deck Turned a Child's Hobby into a High-Stakes, Billion-Dollar Business*. Macmillan General Reference, 1995.

INDEX

G

H

I

J

jobs, 7, 9, 18, 20, 21, 27, 106, 157, 159
  job security, 59
Jobs, Steve, 148

K

Kellogg's, 110, 129
Kentucky Fried Chicken (KFC), 37
key competitors, 3-6, 80, 81, 83, 87, 92, 97, 98, 113, 124
killer products, 4, 88, 108, 109, 123, 124, 126, 128
KISS principle, 129
Kroc, Ray, 37

L

launches, 19, 149
lawsuits. *See* litigation
litigation, 136, 137, 142
Luce, Henry, 23

M

machine gun, 31
management, 16, 35, 44, 45, 57, 61, 68, 74, 75, 92
market, 3, 7, 8, 10,18, 19, 23, 24, 36, 63, 79, 81, 83, 85, 87, 88, 99, 101, 104, 108,
    110, 111, 112, 121, 123, 131, 134, 150, 158, 159
  disasters and mishaps, 108
  Fortune magazine, 23, 59
  key market, 83
  power cords market, 121
  priorities and values, 18
  soft drink market, 85
  software market, 24
  trading cards, 100, 101
  youth market, 85

R

W

Z